Redcar and Coatham

A HISTORY TO THE END OF WORLD WAR II

by

Janet Cockroft

Edited by Peter Sotheran

Line Drawings by M. John Halliwell

Printed and Published by
A. A. SOTHERAN LTD.,
14–16 Queen Street, Redcar, Cleveland.

PUBLISHER'S NOTE

Chapters 1 to 15 of this work were researched and written by Janet Cockroft. The introduction was written by Peter Sotheran who also wrote the paragraphs about the Royal Naval Air Station at Redcar, from notes provided by Gerard Terry. The line drawings, except that of Redcar Parish Church and the 1820 Post Office are by M. John Halliwell. All the photographs are from the publisher's library of local historical prints, contributed by many people of Redcar over recent years.

First published December 1976.

2nd Edition, revised and enlarged, April 1980.

3rd Edition, revised and enlarged, January 1985.

Copyright 1985 A. A. Sotheran Ltd.

No part of this publication may be reproduced, stored in a retrieval system or transmitted in any form or by any means electronic, mechanical, photocopying, recording or otherwise, without the prior permission of the publisher.

Students who make use of this work should acknowledge the title and publisher either in a footnote or a bibliography.

ISBN 0 905032 16 0   0 905032 09 8 (Paperback)

COAT OF ARMS
OF
REDCAR BOROUGH COUNCIL

DESCRIPTION

Barry wavy of six Azure and Argent, a sailing ship proper, pennons flying Gules, in base three fish naiant—two and one—also proper: a chief Sable thereon on a pallet Or, between two steel ingots, a blast furnace, also proper. And for the Crest, on a Wreath of the colours A Lion, rampant and Gules supporting a beacon fired proper.

Motto: Mare et Ferro.

CONTENTS

Coat of Arms of Redcar Borough Council   Frontispiece

INTRODUCTION   In the Beginning . . .   9
    The Conquest; An Ancient Church;
    Kirkleatham Manor

CHAPTER 1   1800–1820   16
    Plan of Redcar; Yeoman's House, Coatham;
    Redcar High Street; Port of Coatham;
    'Zetland' Lifeboat

CHAPTER 2   1821–1840   27
    St. Peter's Church; Wreck of the 'Esk';
    Port William; Wreck of the 'Caroline'

CHAPTER 3   1841–1850   32
    Fishing Industry; The Railway;
    Wreck of the 'Susannah'

CHAPTER 4   1851–1860   36
    Census details; Redcar & Coatham develop;
    Cholera; Redcar Local Board of Health;
    Zetland School

CHAPTER 5   1861–1870   48
    A Visitor's opinion; Three Famous Visitors;
    Revival of Coatham; Coatham Convalescent Home

CHAPTER 6   1870–1875   55
    Census Details; The Ironworks; Warrenby;
    Sacred Heart Church

CHAPTER 7   1876–1880   63
    Kirkleatham & Redcar Local Boards of Health;
    Redcar Racecourse; The Piers

CHAPTER 8   1881–1900   73
    Ordnance Survey Map; Spear's Report;
    Enteric Fever in Coatham; Water Supply;
    Warrenby Boiler Explosion; Two Shipwrecks;
    The Amalgamation

CHAPTER 9   1900–1914 83
   Census Figures; Death of Queen Victoria;
   Dramas at Sea; Coronation of Edward VII;
   The Town Clock; The Town Grows;
   New Public Buildings; Local Justice;
   Saltwater Scheme; Suffragettes;
   Coronation of George V

CHAPTER 10   The Seaside Resort . . . 91
   The Bandstand; On the Beach

CHAPTER 11   1914–1918 97
   On the Home Front; Soldiers in Town;
   Naval Air Station; Peace Celebrations;
   Memorial Tank; War Memorial

CHAPTER 12   1918–1939 104
   Dormanstown; Incorporation of the Borough;
   Gifts to the Borough; Unemployment;
   Three New Roads; New Parks; Locke Park

CHAPTER 13   Housing Development . . . 113
   Temporary Dwellings; First Council Houses;
   Council Building; Private Building;
   Homes for the Aged; Street Names Changed

CHAPTER 14   New Facilities 120
   The Market; Foreshore Control;
   Electricity; The Isolation Hospital;
   Dormanstown School; All Saints' Church;
   Stead Memorial Hospital; Redcar Library;
   'Happy Holidays'; Coatham Enclosure;
   Coronation of George VI

CHAPTER 15   1939–1945 130
   World War II Preparations;
   Redcar at War; Air Raids;
   Re-opening the Beach; Peace in Sight;
   V.E. Day; Aftermath; Political Change

PRINCIPAL EVENTS IN REDCAR . . . 137

CHAIRMEN OF REDCAR URBAN DISTRICT
   COUNCIL SINCE AMALGAMATION . . 140

LIST OF MAYORS 141

LIST OF ILLUSTRATIONS

Coatham Marshes, 1976	Plate 1
Subscribers to the Hearse . . . . Hearse Regulations and Fees	Plate 2
High Street, 1875	Plate 3
The Redcar old lifeboat "Zetland" . .	Plate 4
Esplanade and Newcomen Terrace, 1890 . .	Plate 5
Esplanade, 1890 . . . . . Marsh House Farm, Warrenby, 1926	Plate 6
Coronation Gift — a Tin of Toffees . . The Steam Roundabout on the Beach, 1904	Plate 7
Spence's Victoria Baths, Coatham, 1884 . .	Plate 8
Redcar Pier Head from Steamer Jetty, 1870–1880 . . . . . Coatham Pier, 1875–1880	Plate 9
Coatham Ironworks, Downey & Co., 1890 . Sir Wm. Turner's School (Coatham Grammar School), 1900	Plate 10
Coatham Road, about 1900 . . . Coatham Road, 1st April, 1917	Plate 11
Coatham Enclosure, 1936 . . . . Coatham Enclosure Illuminations, 1937–38	Plate 12

In the Beginning

THE first picture of life in Britain is drawn for us by Julius Caesar. The ancient Britons who fell to the conquering Romans were hunters and farmers. Dressed in coarse woven fabrics, they lived in stone, or wattle and thatch settlements. They tended to be gregarious, keeping in groups of about a score or more, a tribal system. They were fierce, and willing and able to give their all in battle.

With the Romans came civilisation. Sophisticated buildings and organisation supplanted the crude camps of the ancient Britons. In Cleveland the Romans created a line of signal beacons, there was one on Huntcliff. Life for the indigenous natives was still spartan on the coastal plain between the hills and the marshes around the Tees estuary. After some three hundred years of generally good government the Legions withdrew to defend territories nearer to Rome. Unused to liberty and totally unprepared to rule themselves the Britons found themselves in a predicament. The marauding Picts and Scots were able to overrun the country in the north.

Defenceless, after five centuries of Roman protection, the Britons begged the Saxons to help restore order. Hengist and Horsa, sons of a famous Saxon general came to Britain in AD 449. Having sailed up from Kent, the Saxons landed in the north in AD 547 and soon the whole of the lands north of the Humber were in the hands of the Saxons. (There is a difference of opinion here: Bede, writing in the 7th century states that the *Angles* settled Northumbria). The Britons were driven from their own lands, those who remained were enslaved to the Saxons. Although brave and daring fighters, the Saxons at peace were industrious. They tilled the land, kept cattle and lived in permanent settlements. They also brought with them their language, customs and place names. One group settled in the middle of the plain, halfway between Huntcliff and the mouth of the Tees. They called it Mersc after the marshes which covered much of the ground. Popular custom has it that Redcar takes its name from the reeds of the marshes "carr" being a Saxon word for marsh. Over the last 800 years the place has been called "Riedcarre," "Ridekarre," "Reddkerr," "Redcarre," and by 1790, Redcar.

Christianity established under the Romans in 324 AD was banished by the Saxons who placed their faith in Woden. The days of the week which we use today are corruptions of the Saxon gods. Having established themselves, the country existed in comparative peace for two centuries.

A political marriage helped the return of Christianity to the north. To strengthen his position as ruler of Bernica, the land between the Tees and the Forth, Edwin, son of Aella, sought to marry Ethelberga, daughter of Ethelbert, King of Kent. Both king and daughter had been converted to Christianity by the missionary Augustine. The marriage was arranged, conditional on the woman and her attendants being allowed freedom of worship. The monk Paulinus joined the ruler's household as chaplain, and two years later Edwin was converted. He was baptised on Easter Day, 627, in a wooden chapel located where York Minster now stands. Many other nobles turned to Christianity too, among them his niece, Hilda, later to be Abbess of Whitby. A decade later, Saint Aidan, from Iona, came to the area. Monasteries were founded at Whitby and Hartlepool.

A further two centuries passed and the Viking invaders came in force. Although there were Christians amongst them, Christianity waned. Settlements were uprooted and the people driven into the hills. Bloodshed, ravaging and an unsettled way of life returned.

Peace returned under the reign of Athelstan who overthrew the Danish Kingdom at York, in 927 AD. After his death, the Danish king of Dublin restored the northern kingdom in 939 and there followed an unsettled period until the death of Eric Bloodaxe in 954. There was peace for a decade and a half, until 980, followed by further Danish incursions culminating in the great invasion of 1016, after which Knut the Dane became King of England. Christianity was again encouraged and was strengthened by the work of Dunstan and Edward the Confessor, 1042–66. After reigning less than one year Harold II went, and William the Conqueror came. Three years after the Battle of Hastings, the Normans were still at work subduing the Anglo-Saxons. The last resistance came from Edgar the Atheling and a group of northern chiefs which included Gospatric, ancestor of the Marquess of Zetland. The last battle was fought on the marshes at Coatham; the defensive earthworks remained visible until early this century. They are now lost beneath the iron and steel complexes. The Normans won the day and in retaliation put the north of England to the sword and the flame. The Domesday Book records many places as *terrae wastae*—unused lands.

AFTER THE CONQUEST

Ten thousand years ago when the last Ice Age retreated, a forest covered the area from Hartlepool to Whitby and out to the Dogger Bank. The remains of the tree stumps are exposed from time to time when a particular combination of stormy seas and tides scours the sand away from Redcar's central beach, opposite West Terrace. With the Glacial period the seas rose to the present level. The Tees probably entered the sea south of its present estuary, somewhere near Marske. Many wild animals roamed the area. After the Conquest, a Grant, dated 25th May, 1280, was made to Lord Walter De Faucenberg, allowing him a free warren to hunt wild boar, deer, wolf and elk "inn ye forests of Reidkarre."

An ancient market was organised for Coatham as early as 1257. Marmaduke de Thweng procured a King's licence for a market and fair, and although King Edward confirmed the Charter in 1293, there are no records showing the success or failure of the venture. The saltworks at Coatham had existed for some six hundred years by this time.

AN ANCIENT CHURCH

Much research was done into the history of an old chapel amongst the Coatham sandbanks by Thomas McAll Fallow, M.A., F.S.A. He had retired to Coatham in 1872 and was an active member of the parish church and served on several public bodies. The chapel probably stood near to Marsh House Farm, in the shadow of the Redcar Steel Complex. Mrs. Faith, who had lived at the farm as a child in the first half of the nineteenth century, knew of the chapel and remembered seeing the remains of the walls near the farm. Stones were removed from the walls to repair outbuildings of the farmhouse. A Mr. Suggett remembered finding several skulls and other remains while digging in the vicinity of the chapel site, at the same period as Mrs. Faith. A prominent sandhill, immediately north-east of the farm was known as "Church Hill" from its proximity to the chapel.

The earliest written reference to the chapel occurred in the will of Robert Taylor of East Coatham, dated 5th October, 1470; twelve pence (5p) was bequeathed towards the repair of the chapel of Saint Sulpitius. Another man of East Coatham made his will on 10th December, 1473. In it he bequeathed his soul "to God the Father Almighty, to Blessed Mary, and to all the Saints," and directed his body to be buried within the chapel of Saint Sulpitius in the parish of Kirkleatham, which at that time, of course extended to the sea. He went on to endow the living with the income from rents of various specified lands and tenements in Kirkleatham, Upleatham and Seaton Carew; this endowment was conditional on the inhabitants obtaining a Royal Licence which would enable the chapel to become parochial in its own right. Since Coatham remained a part of Kirkleatham Parish until the nineteenth century it was a dream never realised. William Raughton (or Raughtonbald) in his will around 1500, left to "Saint Syplyn A nawter clothe and a Kandylstik" — an altar cloth and candlestick; this testament was written in English. There are other references to the chapel during the 16th century.

In 1545 an Act of Parliament was passed empowering Henry VIII to dissolve the many religious establishments throughout the country and seize their property; the proceeds were to defray the costs of the French and Scottish wars. Commissioners were employed to enquire into the nature of their property and income. The Commissioners for Yorkshire presented the following report, dated 14th February, 1547:

"The Chapell called Sepulchres Chapell in the Paryshe of Kyrkelethome. William Arnarde Incumbent there of thaige fforty yeres of honeste conversacion and qualities and of good lerneninge, having no other promocions but only the revenewe of the said chauntery or chapel. The necessitie of the said chapell is to do divine service to the inhabitaunts there, being distaunt frome the parishes churche twoo myles, and there is in the said parishe of howselling people (communicants) to the number of cccxii (312) and there is no landes ne tenements sold sithens the said xxiii day of November in the year of the reign of the late King Henry VIII the thirty-seventh (1546). "The yerely value of said chapell is as shall appere by the particulars of sayme, xlvij s. iiij d. (£2·36) Summa of the said chapel xlvij s. iiij d. which remain."

In 1575, Queen Elizabeth I issued a Commission of Inquiry into certain "concealed lands," as they were called, in Yorkshire. Of Kirkleatham, the Commissioners reported the folowing:

"And also that there is a free chapel wih appurtenances and a yard belonging to it in the parish of Kirkleadam, otherwise called Seplyns Chapell, in the said County of York, the land containing by estimation one acre more or less, now or lately in the tenure or occupation of Christopher Marshall or his assigns. And also that there are twelve swathes of grass in Este and Weste Coatham Inges in Cleveland . . . and appropriated for one priest called the Chauntrie Priest (of) the Chapel of Seplyns."

East and West Coatham Ings were land around Marsh House Farm, particularly to the south and west of it. It is possible that the farm house is on the site of, and may comprise parts of, the residence of these early chaplains at Coatham.

The next reference to the chapel is in the thirteenth year of Elizabeth I (1578) when an indenture was enrolled in chancery by which Edmund Downynge and Milo Doddinge, both notorious land jobbers of London, sold to Richard Bellasis of Morton, Durham, all "le frontland" containing half an acre, and the arable lands at Kirkleatham which had belonged to the late Chantry of "St. Sulphon." Frontland or frontsted was a term applied to a site on which a house or other building stood. From the Bellasis family, the manor of Kirkleatham with this piece of church property passed by purchase to John Turner of Guisborough. More of the Turners and their successors presently.

In a conveyance dated 9th July, 1632, Robert Coulthirst (whose fine memorial brass is still in Kirkleatham church) assigned to John Turner some lands in East Coatham, including "one parcel of ground called . . . Kirkhill . . . adjoining East Coatham coney warren." The Church Hill was levelled and removed around the time that the railway reached Redcar in the early 1800's.

Five variations of name were given to the chapel; St. Sulpitius, St. Seplyn, St. Sulphon, Sepulchre's, St. Cyprian. An early correspondent wrote (Cotton Manuscripts, British Museum):

> 'They have a tradycion that the Danes used to land there (at Dabholm, as Coatham was then called) showing great heapes of bones in the sands . . . whether they had got a crust or noe, or that there were shome charnell house there I know not, wch I suspecte by a reason that a chapell . . . is neare at hand."

The allusion to a charnel house in connection with the chapel is interesting and instructive in that it affords a clue to the origin of the name of Sepulchre's Chapel. St. Seplyn's and St. Sulphon are manifest errors on the part of some copyist. In interpreting place names, the oldest form usually gives the best clue to the origin. Sulpitius was the earliest, and is a quite reasonable dedication for a chapel; a chapel at York Minster bore the same dedication before the Reformation. The Coatham chapel may well have served as a burial-place for sailors washed up on the beaches and thus became known as the Sepulchre Chapel. St. Sulphon was probably a contraction of Sulpitius. St. Cyprian was probably a conjectured correction of Seplyn.

The building itself was probably small and without any architectural distinction. The windows would have slightly pointed heads possibly with pierced stones. It is doubtful if there was anything to divide the sanctuary from the nave of the church. There may have been a bell gable at the west end. From the bequests for repairs in the fifteenth century, it is apparent that there was work to be done; the building may even have been altered somewhat to the prependicular style of that century. A small porch may have been added to the entrance in the south side.

KIRKLEATHAM MANOR

Kirkleatham takes its name from an Anglo-Saxon word "hlipum" meaning a slope. The "Kirk" prefix was added and subtracted through the centuries to distinguish the village from Upleatham.

Robert de Brus was granted one of the Kirkleatham manors, along with other manors in the north after the Domesday Survey. The other manor was held by the Perci's and was 'let' by them to the de Kilton family, along with the manor of Kilton, as one Knight's fee. It passed by marriage to the de Thweng family and was settled on Marmaduke, younger son of Marmaduke de Thweng and his wife Lucy de Brus. In the fourteenth century it passed to the Lumley family, in 1375 by marriage.

The manor was sold by the last Lord Lumley in June, 1586, for 200 marks to Thomas Crompton and Edmund Hunt. Afterwards it became the property of Richard Bellasis and at his death at the turn of the century, it passed to his nephews Charles and Brian Bellasis successively. Charles died in 1601 and Brian in 1608, leaving a son and heir William, from whom, in January, 1623-4 the manor of Kirkleatham was bought by John Turner. From him, it descended in 1643 to his eldest son John Turner, who died in 1688. He was succeeded by his son Charles, who was followed in 1719, by his son Cholmley. In 1757 Cholmley died without succeding male issue and the manor of Kirkleatham passed to his brother William and thence to William's son Charles, who in 1782 was created a baronet. Sir Charles Turner, the second baronet, inherited the manor from his father in 1783 and, dying childless in 1810, willed it to his wife Teresa, daughter of Sir William Gleadowe-Newcomen.

In 1812 Lady Turner married Henry Vansittart of Foxley. She died in 1844, leaving an only child Teresa Vansittart. In 1841 Teresa married Arthur Newcomen and on the death of her stepfather she became owner of the manor in 1848. Mrs. Newcomen was succeded in 1867 by her son Arthur Henry Turner Newcomen and he in 1884 by his son Gleadowe Henry Turner Newcomen. Gleadhowe never married and at his death, Kathleen Teresa Turner Newcomen succeeded to the estate in 1932. Kathleen had married Colonel Le Roy Lewis and they had one son and four daughters. On the death of Mrs. Le Roy Lewis, the estate passed to the son, Henry. The following year, 1949, he sold the house to Ortem Estates and the land to another company. The hospital eventually passed through the hands of the Charity Commissioners to a Board of Trustees.

CHAPTER ONE — 1800 - 1820

AT the beginning of the nineteenth century, Redcar and Coatham were two quite separate villages a mile apart. Coatham was in the parish of Kirkleatham, Redcar was mainly in the parish of Marske although a small portion of the village belonged to the parish of Upleatham.

Upleatham controlled a square portion on the foreshore at the east end of the village. How this came about is not absolutely clear, it seems likely that the manor at Upleatham held certain fishing rights at Redcar and that these were secured by the attachment of the land to Upleatham parish. The boundary between the parishes of Marske and Kirkleatham ran along the present West Dyke Road.

Coatham was part of the Kirkleatham Estate and, as such, it belonged to the Turner family at Kirkleatham Hall who had purchased it in 1623. Redcar was part of the Marske Estate, owned by the Dundas family, having been purchased by Sir Lawrence Dundas in 1762. His grandson also called Lawrence was created Earl of Zetland in 1838 and the title is perpetuated by the family who still maintain many interests around Marske-by-Sea and live at Aske, near Richmond, Yorkshire.

The first national census was taken in 1801. Redcar is recorded as consisting of 115 inhabited houses containing 125 families. There were 170 males and 261 females. That the females greatly outnumbered the males could be partially explained by the fact that as many of the men were seafarers there was always a great number away from home.

This first census included Coatham with the rest of the parish of Kirkleatham. The population of the whole parish was 680 living in 159 houses. The population of Coatham would be about half of this, or a little less.

TOTAL POPULATION FIGURES

Census	Redcar	Kirkleatham
1801	431	680
1811	411	622
1821	673	686

The population of Redcar decreased during the first decade of the century for no particular reason, then in the following decade it increased by 50 per cent. Kirkleatham also suffered a decrease but later recovered its losses although without a dramatic increase as at Redcar. Coincidental with the lower census returns, Europe was in the throes of the Napoleonic Wars. It is feasible that many seafaring men were involved in the navy. As Redcar continued to grow as a resort, Kirkleatham's population remained almost static for the following forty years.

In his book *The History of Cleveland,* published in 1808, Revd. Graves described Redcar as "a considerable fishing town situated close upon the beach". He adds that Redcar "consisted formerly of a few miserable huts only, inhabited by fishermen and their families; but is now a place of fashionable resort for sea-bathing." Redcar was visited during the summer months by genteel families from the surrounding countryside. The number of lodging houses increased each year and Graves found them to be "neat and commodious". As a visitor to the town, he was surprised to see heaps of drift sand nearly as high as the cottages!

Coatham was similar, though quieter, and in Graves' opinion—superior, more suited to cater for invalids seeking the bracing sea air than was Redcar which he rated as a poorer community. Graves also came upon "a large and commodious inn". This was the original Lobster Inn, built some years earlier by Charles Turner who had done much to improve the amenities and roads of the area. Graves seems to have enjoyed his stay in the two resorts as he praised their gentility and simplicity. Indeed he wished that the "innocent enjoyments of Coatham might be found in other watering places instead of the passion for gambling."

In 1810 was published Hutton's celebrated *A Trip to Coatham.* W. Hutton journeyed to Coatham from Birmingham at the age of 86, with his invalid daughter who, he hoped, would benefit from the sea air. A distinguished antiquarian, he took a great interest in Redcar and Coatham, declaring, "I shall have the honour of being their first historian".

He described Redcar and Coatham as two hamlets which "an age back could have been no more than small fishing places, which, instead of being known one hundred miles off, were scarcely known by their neighbours". They were in fact two small villages separated by an open green. Coatham was a single street built along the south side only; Hutton estimates that there were around seventy houses. Redcar was also a single street, built on both north and south sides and consisted of one hundred and fifteen houses.

The mountains of drift sand covering the streets were still a feature of the villages and made walking difficult. Hutton jokes "no carriage above a wheelbarrow ought to venture". In some places the sandbanks came right up to the eaves of the cottages and doorways needed clearing each day. A century ahead of the event, Hutton approved the principle of an amalgam of the two neighbouring villages, believing that it would benefit both places. Times were untroubled. There was no constable stationed in the fishing villages and according to Hutton, there was no need for one. The people were clean and well-mannered and the children well-kept. He did not see a single "ragged person".

The sea was the mainstay of life for many. Coatham had about a dozen cobles and Redcar twenty-eight. As well as fish the sea yielded sea-coal, both were used by the locals themselves and also resold. From the twentieth century we must wonder at the panorama of the seascape with upwards of fifty sailing ships passing between Hartlepool and Huntcliff each day.

Both Redcar and Coatham were quiet watering places. Amusements were simple. Visitors were content with the beach and bracing air during the day and a game of cards at night. No doubt they also took outings to the pleasant unspoilt villages in the neighbourhood. The roads were remarkably fine for the time, suitable for walking, riding, or travelling by carriage. The sea was the main attraction. Excursion parties would take to the sea for three or four hours, sailing down to Saltburn and back, or across the bay to Seaton where they might disembark for tea before returning. There was also a lending library and for a few years a small theatre. As the century progressed local entrepreneurs catered more and more for the visitors. Bicycles, tricycles and baby-carriages could be hired by the hour or day. By prior arrangement, the guest-houses would have a pianoforte installed for your amusement.

The sea-bathing was what the visitors really sought. Coatham had four bathing machines and Redcar a dozen. Public bathing was still a new idea and had yet to be approved of in higher social circles. The sparsity of bathing machines at Coatham was in keeping with its image as the more socially acceptable of the two resorts. The price of a 'dip' from a bathing machine was around one shilling. There were also facilities for warm water bathing, rather expensive at three shillings and sixpence a time. Compare those charges with the cost of lodgings. A family could rent a suite of rooms or a whole house for between two and five guineas per week. Hutton detailed the daily expenses for himself and his invalid daughter when they stayed at the Public Hotel.

For each person	4s. 6d.
For the coachman	3s.
For each of the two horses . . .	3s.

PLAN OF REDCAR 1815

AT this time Redcar consisted of one street—the High Street— and comprised one hundred and fifteen houses and three inns. On the south side there were sixty-two houses, most of which had long gardens behind them. The fishermen would keep a few hens, perhaps a pig and grow a few vegetables. Some houses are shown with small outbuildings at the end of the plots. These were often the bait-houses where fishing tackle was kept and prepared. Some of these little buildings still survive amongst the commercial property backing on to Lord Street. There was also the Red Lion Inn, an old-established inn with stables immediately behind it, across Lord Street. On the North side there were forty-eight houses, some of which had long gardens running down to the beach. The other two inns were on this side, the Swan and the Ship Inn. Five more houses stood in the middle of the thoroughfare. Along the sea front were the gardens, yards and offices of the High Street traders. The only building was the lifeboat house.

At the western end of the village was the first Zetland School, built in 1807. The school, with a house for the master, was built and endowed by Sir Lawrence Dundas, first Earl of Zetland, who lived at Upleatham Hall. The master was to teach ten children free of charge and was restricted to a charge of not more than four shillings a quarter for the instruction of the children of pilots and labourers. The old school was used for fifty years until the present Zetland School was built, near Redcar Parish Church. It stood in what is now West Terrace, on a site presently occupied by the office of an Estate Agent. Next to the school stood the Methodist Meeting House. This was the first place of worship in Redcar and remained the only one until the building of St. Peter's Parish Church in 1829. From Hutton's comments we learn that the Methodist Meetings were always well attended.

In 1815 there were two bath houses, very necessary in those days before the advent of sanitation and concern for personal hygiene amongst the 'working classes'. One establishment was run by Mr.

Carter; the other being Stamps's baths. Their positions are indicated on the Plan of 1815. Later there were to be Spence's and Skinner's Baths. The latter was established by the grandfather of Charles Skinner who was known by two generations of Redcar youngsters as he ran the Model Shop in Station Road and latterly on the Esplanade. Skinner's baths were on Lord Street opposite the Police Station. Mr. Spence's establishment was between Cleveland Street and the Esplanade.

The Poor House consisted of two cottages, which as the name tells, were used 'for the reception of the poor'. This was prior to the building of the Workhouse at Guisborough. This latter establishment became part of Guisborough General Hospital.

At this time, Redcar was part of the ecclesiastical parish of Marske. The old church of St. Germain was the parish church and was usually reached by the cliff-top paths or by carriage, via Redcar Lane and Redcar Road at Marske; at times of low water, the direct route was on to the beach at Granville Terrace, Redcar and up Spout Chine (the Valley Gardens) at Marske. A parish hearse was provided for funerals of people from Redcar. It was kept in the Hearse House, situated at the rear of 151 and 153 High Street. Parts of this property survive today virtually unchanged.

The rules for the use of the Parish Hearse stipulated that it was not to travel more than twenty miles from Redcar and that the innkeeper who took it away was responsible for it and for collecting the hire fares. The hearse was bought by public subscription in 1812 and 102 people contributed to its cost. Subscribers could expect one free journey, others paid as follows: Stokesley 10s. 6d., Guisborough and Ormesby 6s., Wilton 4s., Skelton 5s., Kirkleatham 3s. 6d. Between Redcar and Marske the 'fare' was 2s. 6d., Coatham to Marske 3s. 6d.

One name which appears on the list of householders accompanying the old town plan is that of Fleck. James Fleck married Margaret, sister of Captain James Cook, R.N., the circumnavigator. Margaret had been living at Redcar, with her father, also a James Cook, at the time. Captain Cook was killed in Hawaii, February 14th, 1779. His father, a day labourer, died at Redcar on April 1st of the same year. Margaret, wife of James Fleck, died on 9th August, 1798, aged 26 years. Her husband, a master mariner like her brother, died April 20th, 1828, aged 64. Several of the family, including Captain Cook's father, are buried in St. Germain's churchyard at Marske.

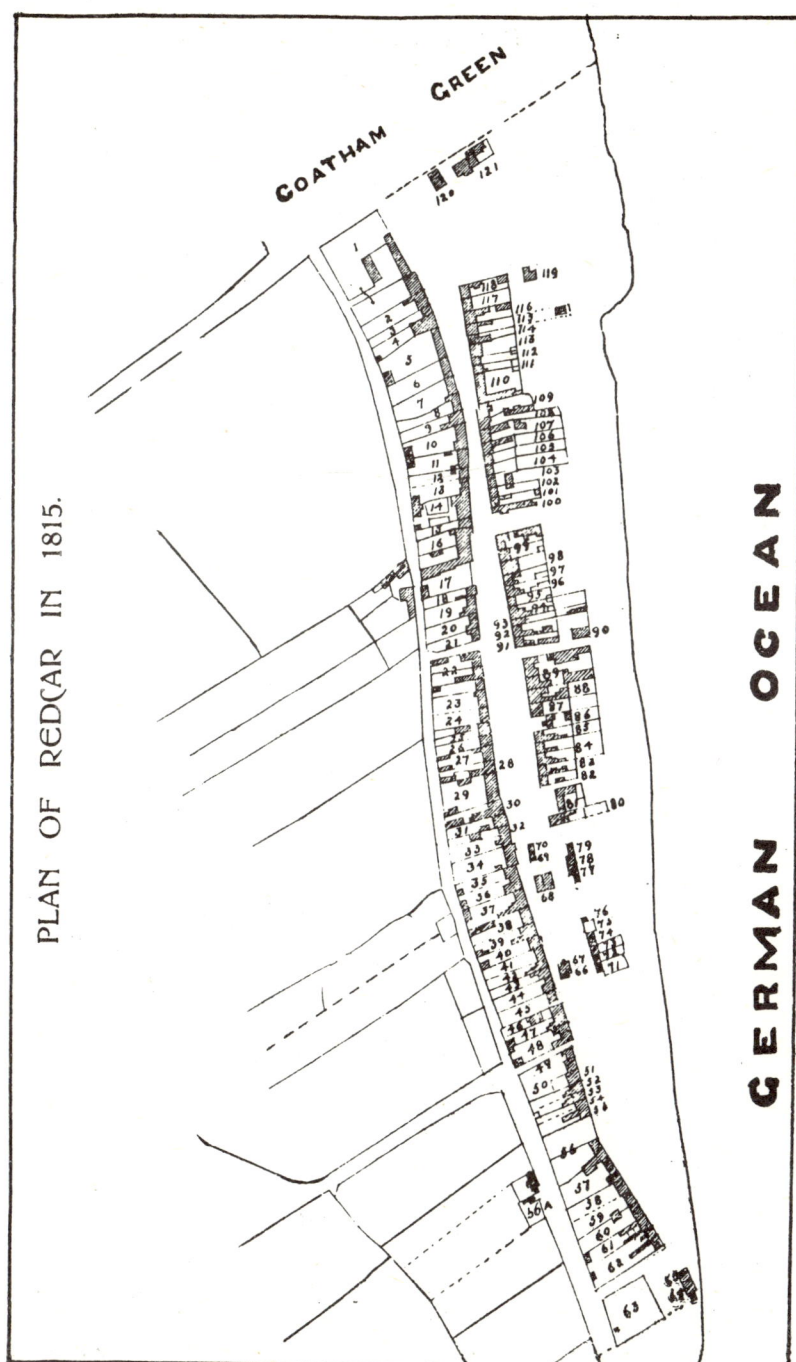

KEY TO THE PLAN OF REDCAR

HOUSES, Etc., ON SOUTH SIDE
Note: H—House; G—Garden

1. Messrs. Foster and Duck, H. G. &c.
2. Zachariah Gardener, H & G
3. Mary Boagy, H and G
4. Thomas Rudd, H and G
5. Robert Henderson, H.
6. Widow Pignette, H and G
7. Tho. Mill, H and G
8. Mary Davison, H and Yard
9. James Henderson, H and G
10. Wm. Clement, H and G and Stackyard
11. Joseph Dove, H and G
12. Ann Allan, H and G
13. Robert Simpson, H and G
14. Messrs. Foster and Duck, H, G, &c.
15. Ralph Greensides, H and G
16. Mrs. Carlton, Inn and Offices
17. Joseph Fenwick, Barn and Garth
18. Tho. Thompson, H & G
19. { Dorothy Andrew, H and G
    { Geo. Robinson, H & G
20. Elizabeth Walton, H and Garth
21. Robert Barker, H and G
22. Wm. Smith, H and G
23. Tho. Burnegal, H and G
24. Tho. Burnegal, H and G
25. Wm. Marfleet, H and G
26. Margt. Potts, H and G
27. Margaret Dowton, H and G
28. Margt. Wilson, H and G
29. Mrs. Law, H and G
30. Wm. Johnson, H and G
31. Slater Potts, H and G
32. John Dobson, H and G
33. John Dobson, senr., H and G
34. William Potts, H and G
35. William Bladderwick
36. Tho. Hall, H and G
37. Jonathan Milner, H and G
38. William Webster, H and G
39. Rev. Mr. Saul, H and G
40. James Lynas, H and G
41. Thos. Thompson, H and G
42. Peter Walton, H and G
43. Tho. Thompson, H and G
44. Wm. Thompson, H and G
45. Wm. Guy, H and G
46. Dorothy Potts, H and G
47. William Johnson, H and G
48. John Busby, H and G
49. Palister Thompson, H and G
50. John Carlton, H and G
51. John Spurr, H and G
52. Mary Watson, H and G
53. Robert Burnegal, H and G
54. William Bladderwick
55. James Fleck, H and G
56. Tho. Agar, H, Garth, &c.
56a. John Trattles, H and G
57. John Eden, H and G
58. Tho. Robson, H and G
59. Simpson Adamson, H and G
60. Mrs. Agar, H and G
61. John Brown, H and G
62. Rev. Jos. Smith, H and G
63. Richard Dobson, G
64. Richard Dobson, H
65. Richard Dobson, H
66. Chr. Robinson, H
67. John Crane, H
68. Jonathan Milner, H and G } In the middle of the Street
69. Thos. Hall, H
70. William Potts, H

HOUSES Etc. ON NORTH SIDE

71. Josh. Pounder, H and G
72. Tho. Hall, H and G
73. James Fleck, H and G
74. Poor Houses
75. The Pinfold
76. The Hearse House
77. Mary Graham, H
78. Mary Carlton, H
79. Tho. Robinson, H
80. John Hutton, H and G
81. { Robt. Boagy, H and Yard
    { John Dobson, jun. H and Yard
    { Tho. Bilton, H and Yard
82. Ralph Greensides, H and G
83. Mr. Bell, H and G
84. Margt. Wilson, 2 Houses & Offices
85. Thos. Fleck, H and G
86. Mary Davison, H and G
87. Malcolm McNaughton, H and G
88. Tho. Thompson, H and G
89. John Eden, Inn, House & Offices
90. Lifeboat House
91. Geo. Johnson, H. Offices &c.
92. Chr. Moor, H. and Offices
93. Tho. Walton, H etc.
94. John Walton, H etc.
95. Margt. Waistal, H etc.
96. Saml. Richley, H etc.
97. Ralph Carter, H etc.
98. John Richley, H etc.
99. Jas. Carter, 2 Houses & Offices
100. Jas. Carter, H, Baths, &c.
101. William Smith, H and Offices
102. Eliz. Clarke, House etc.
103. Thos. Potts, H and G
104. W. Webster, H and G
105. Joseph Dove, H and G
106. Alice Potts, H etc.
107. John Thwaites, H etc.
108. Esther Darnton, H etc.
109. Joseph Barnett, H and G
110. Mrs. Carlton, 2 Houses and G
111. James Lynas, H and Offices
112. Ann Winn, H and Office
113. Ann Stamp, H etc.
114. Mr. Horner, H etc.
115. John Barnett, H etc.
116. John Spurr, H and G
117. John Wilkinson, H etc.
118. Mary Hull, H etc.
119. Geo. Stamp, Baths
120. Soc. of Methodists' Meeting House
121. School House and Yard

Part of Upleatham

THE BUILDINGS

ONE or two of the oldest cottages were cruck built. The main structure of the building was carried by huge 'A' frames, usually either three, or five in larger buildings which would also accommodate some livestock. The frames were erected in a row, forming a tent-like structure. With the tops linked to form the ridge, the crossbars were joined and crude walls of local materials—rocks, stones, or clay filled in up to the level of the crossbars, usually six or seven feet above the ground. The earliest of the dwellings were thatched. As the eighteenth century turned into the nineteenth, red tiles predominated.

The smaller cruck houses had a central passageway from the entrance, at right angles to the length of the building; one side would be living quarters, the other work space or sleeping quarters. In later years, the cross-members of the frames were boarded across to make a loft, either for storage or sleeping. The longer, five cruck, houses would be divided roughly into one-third and two-thirds. The smaller portion was the living quarters and was separated from the larger end by a passage-way which crossed the house from wall to wall with entrances at either side. These larger buildings predominated in rural areas and the larger portion accommodated the smallholder's livestock. Before lofts were made, smoke from a central hearth escaped through a smoke hole or the eaves; later chimneys were incorporated.

Redcar's original post office functioned for some years, from around 1820 in a cruck house. It was located between the Red Lion Inn and the west end of the High Street. The last of the ancient cruck houses in Redcar was demolished in 1911. "Old Pott's Cottage" as it was known, stood at 118 High Street where there is now a solicitor's office. This cottage was recorded in a census taken during the reign of Henry VIII (1509-1547). When it was demolished, a smuggler's 'dark cupboard' or gin-cupboard was discovered.

The overall appearance of the cottages was one of cleanliness and good order. In front of many, on their seaward side, were low buildings which served dual purposes as outhouses and as barriers to the wind-blown sand.

THE YEOMAN'S HOUSE, COATHAM

BUILT in 1698, and standing in Coatham High Street, it is the oldest surviving house in the town and one of the oldest in Cleveland. Along with the date of its construction, the builder placed above the door the initials of the man and woman who first owned the house. The original house is now divided into two dwellings. The real front door was that under the engraved lintel. A small oval window nearby was the "fire window" which allowed light on to the hearth, which was otherwise in considerable shadow because of the large smoke hood. The original stone mullions make the other windows worthy of interest also.

REDCAR HIGH STREET

A NUMBER of handsome middle-class houses were built along the High Street during the later years of the eighteenth century. A good example is number 44, built in 1772 and now part of Boots shop. Another building well preserved above its commercial frontage is that of Greenwood's Menswear at number 47, built in 1778. Probably the oldest building is 98 High Street, now occupied by an insurance company. It is a neat three storeyed house, thought to have been built in the seventeenth century. At the side of the property is a narrow passage leading to Lord Street.

Several large buildings, now public houses, were the superior homes of the eighteenth century. The Stockton Hotel was built before 1703 and at that time was owned by Mrs. Mary Hall and Ann Blatherwick as their dwelling. The "Crown and Anchor" was demolished and rebuilt about 1967. Its predecessor with the same name was built as a private house in 1778. Regulars at the old "Crown and Anchor" remember with affection the tiny rooms, the cosy fireplaces and the narrow passages through the building.

The oldest document referring to the Red Lion Inn is dated 1761. Occupied by John Skirton, farmer, it was almost certainly a farmhouse. By the beginning of the nineteenth century it was a popular inn. The age of the building is readily discerned from the rear access. In the cobbled yard are a mounting block and stables. Extensive stables adjacent to the rear of the hotel, across Lord Street were used as a riding school during this century until their closure in the 1970s. The Swan Hotel, previously an inn, can also be traced back to the eighteenth century.

One of the finest remaining buildings of the early nineteenth century is 151 High Street. It is again a three storeyed house with original sash windows and a pilastered doorway. One distinctive style occurring in many buildings of this period is the long window with a semi-circular head over the landing halfway up the stairs. These are still obvious at the rear of several nearby properties in the High Street.

THE PORT OF COATHAM

DURING the first decade of the nineteenth century, Coatham was still a small port and it belonged to the Kirkleatham Estate. In 1778, Charles Turner appointed John Agar, a yeoman of Coatham, "to collect the duties of anchorage, groundage and beaconage". Between 1789 and 1808 John Agar, kept a record of the movement of the ships and the monies he collected. (The note book is preserved at the North Yorkshire County Record Office). Many of the ships putting in to Coatham were from Sunderland, Hartlepool, Stockton and Whitby. Their cargoes were mainly coal, lime and building materials; they unloaded at the water's edge and the goods were hauled across the sands. Other vessels anchored off Coatham to await a favourable wind to carry them up the Tees to the ports of Yarm or Stockton and later to Middlesbrough.

In 1808 the Tees Navigation Company was created by Act of Parliament and thus the Turner family lost rights to the shipping dues. The Tees was about to become a major port. At the time the Navigation Company was founded, Middlesbrough was still a farm with a derelict priory; Newport, Linthorpe and Acklam were separate villages. With the development of Stockton's port in 1825, Yarm declined. When the railways arrived at Middlesbrough three years later, trade again moved down the river. The earliest coal staithes were at Port Clarence in 1844 and Port Darlington, adjacent to the end of what is now Linthorpe Road in 1830. The development of the coal and later the iron industries needed these more efficient port facilities, consequently, the port of Coatham declined very rapidly.

THE " ZETLAND " LIFEBOAT

THE oldest surviving lifeboat in the world is preserved in Redcar. She was built at South Shields in 1800 by Henry Greathead and originally stationed at Spurn Point in the Humber Estuary. However, she did not see much active service and was offered for sale. The fishermen of Redcar bought her for £100 and named her "Zetland". The boathouse was given by Lord Zetland and was situated close to the beach on the site of the present lifeboat station.

When the boat was called out, a boy was sent round the town beating a drum to summon the crew. Men and women would strain together to wheel the boat across the beach to the sea. Later a rocket maroon was used to call out the crew and the boat hauled by horses in to the water. A specially trained team of eight horses were kept at Ings Farm. On hearing the rocket's explosion, the farmer released the horses and they galloped down Redcar Lane on their own, often arriving before the crew. The "Zetland" arrived at Redcar in 1802. Between then and her final withdrawal from service in 1880, she saved over 500 lives.

CHAPTER TWO — 1821 - 1840

THE 1820's were to find Redcar growing in popularity as a sea-bathing resort. At the same time its fishing activities were flourishing. The market for Redcar fish extended inland beyond the immediately neighbouring communities.

Baine's Yorkshire, one of the earliest directories was compiled in 1823. The information in the directory reflects the growing importance of Redcar. One is struck by the number of shopkeepers and craftsmen in the village. As well as several grocers, drapers and shoemakers, there were jewellers, milliners, a hairdresser and even a straw-bonnet maker. Alongside their main trade, many shops dealt in a wide range of other goods; it would seem curious today to find a shoemaker who was also a tea dealer. Five inns were listed in the directory, the "Jolly Sailor" and the "Crown and Anchor" being the recent additions. There were twenty-five lodging house keepers and many other people took in paying guests during the season. It is also recorded that a few gentlefolk had found a quiet retreat in Redcar, or taken up residence to benefit from the clean, bracing air. Redcar was clearly thriving.

The rival resort of Coatham, a mile away, was losing popularity as a resort by the 1820's. In his *Dictionary of Towns, Hamlets and Villages of Yorkshire,* Thomas Langdale comments, "Few people now resort to Coatham for bathing because it is further from the sea than Redcar". Bain's directory does not record any lodging houses and still only one inn. We conclude that with the demise of its port, Coatham had remained a small hamlet and was reverting to its agricultural living.

Visitors to the area travelled by coach or carriage. During the season, a coach ran three times a week from Bedale. It travelled via Northallerton, Stokesley and Guisborough and was known as "The Cleveland". Alternate journeys the coach rested at the Red Lion and Swan inns. From Northallerton there was a connection with the Leeds coach.

Besides the old Zetland school in West Terrace, there was a small private school, or "Academy" as it styled itself. At Coatham there was a small free school "for the education of fifty poor children". This school had been established by the Turner family of Kirkleatham Hall, in 1811. Twelve of the children were given a suit of clothes each year.

ST. PETER'S CHURCH

DESPITE Redcar's growing importance and rising population, the only place of worship was the Methodist Chapel. Church of England members were expected to attend the old church of St. Germain at Marske. For hundreds of years, funeral processions from Redcar had walked three miles along the beach to Marske. The coffin was carried by bearers, the mourners singing hymns as they walked behind. The cortège would wind its way up from the beach by the "Corpse Path". The coffin would be set down by the wayside cross on the edge of the Headlands opposite Cliff House at Marske for a while. When the bearers were rested the procession would move slowly along the last half-mile of cliff-top path to St. Germain's Church. The alternative route was via Redcar Lane in the Parish Hearse.

In 1821 St. Germain's was in a dilapidated state and was demolished and rebuilt but could no longer accommodate the many summer visitors. In 1823, a petition was sent to the Justices of the Peace at Northallerton stating:

> "That the inhabitants of Redcar who, together with those of the adjoining village of Coatham, amount to one thousand souls, exclusive of five hundred visitors who resort there during the bathing season, are desirous of attending public worship . . . but are unable to do so from the impossibility of accommodation in the parish church, and on account of its great distance."

Later that year, the foundation stone of St. Peter's Church was laid. However, funds were not sufficient for its completion for a further six years. It was consecrated by the Archbishop of York in 1829. The church has been described as a standing monument to the benevolence of the Zetland family. The Earl of Zetland gave the land for the site, the stone for the building and a handsome donation besides. The Church Building Society contributed £500 and the balance was raised by public subscription.

St. Peter's Parish Church is a plain stone building with a small tower. The turrets on the tower are a useful landmark for local fishermen, guiding them through the Saltscar rocks. Inside, the original building was typical of its time, being furnished with box pews (removed in 1888). The original seating accommodated seven hundred people; four hundred and eighty seats were free, the remainder were rented to the wealthier families. Within twenty years the continuing growth of the town necessitated extensions to the building. The first priest-in-charge was the vicar of Upleatham; he travelled between his churches on a donkey.

The communities of Redcar and Marske would have been much the poorer without the generous provisions of the Zetlands. The original village school on West Terrace had been provided by Lawrence Dundas, Earl of Zetland; other buildings included the lifeboat house, the present Zetland School adjacent to St. Peter's church. At Marske the family provided two schools, St. Mark's Parish Church and the Village Institute. In this century the present Marquis of Zetland presented Marske Hall to the Leonard Cheshire Foundation Homes for Sick.

THE WRECK OF THE " ESK "

THE Yorkshire coast is a dangerous one in times of gales and storms. There is no readily accessible refuge harbour between the Humber and the Tyne. Entering Whitby was impossible when running before a storm in a sailing ship. The rocks at Redcar claimed many boats and countless lives.

Seventy-three boats were wrecked off Redcar in the winter of 1820, and over thirty were wrecked or beached in one storm. One of the most tragic was the fate of the *Esk*, a whaler of 345 tons. Leaving the Tyne with only light winds, the captain hugged the shore to take advantage of the prevailing tidal currents. Returning from the waters off Greenland, Captain Dunbar was anxious to make his home port of Whitby. An on-shore gale sprang up on 7th September, 1826 and drove the whaler across the rocks to the east of Redcar. The boat ran ashore and quickly broke up. From the shore, watchers saw five or six men grasping at each piece of floating wreckage. Only three survived from the crew of twenty-nine.

THE PORT WILLIAM HARBOUR SCHEME

THERE was public concern at the lack of a safe anchorage along this hazardous coast. In 1833, Mr. William Richmond put forward the case for building a refuge harbour at Redcar. A public subscription was then started in the town to further this aim.

The scheme was the work of Mr. W. A. Brookes, a civil engineer from Stockton on Tees. After surveying the coast he found that the very rocks which had hitherto been such a hazard for shipping might form the natural base for a harbour. According to his scheme, the two parallel ridges of rock, Eastscar and Saltscar, would be extended a little further out to sea. Piers of solid stone could then be built along them, forming a sheltered harbour of 530 acres. The piers would project about one and a quarter miles out to sea; the entrance would be a thousand yards wide and thirty feet deep at low water. It would accommodate a fleet of Line of Battle ships or over two hundred coastal vessels. The obvious advantage of the scheme was that nature had done all the preparatory work in providing the foundations. Brookes estimated that the northern defence wall would cost £160,000 and the whole work £300,000. He also envisaged the provision of a third wall to the east of the Eastscar rocks thus making a second basin which would be reserved for naval vessels. The harbour was to be named "Port William" in honour of the reigning monarch.

The Bill for Port William was introduced to Parliament in 1839. It immediately met strong opposition from the Stockton M.P.s who feared, perhaps rightly, that Stockton would lose trade to Redcar. One of the most contentious clauses in the Bill was that causing a tonnage rate to be levied on all loaded vessels passing the port. The argument was that in times of storm, any passing vessel would be grateful for the port's existence, and the levy would also help defray the building costs. This clause was the undoing of the Bill and it was subsequently lost.

Twenty years later there was a further attempt to implement the Port William scheme. This time it was intended that the Port be linked with Middlesbrough by a ship canal to be cut through the Coatham Marshes. This would do away with the dangerous passage through the shoals of the wide Tees estuary and shorten the distance to Middlesbrough where the infant iron industry was growing at a prodigious pace. Again the scheme came to nothing. In 1859 came the report of the Harbour of Refuge Commissioners. They recommended the construction of three harbours; one at the entrance of the Tyne, one at Filey, and the other at Hartlepool. In preferring Hartlepool, the report stated:

> "Redcar, a place without trade or great commercial interests can contribute nothing to the expense of a harbour, whereas from Hartlepool, a flourishing port of daily increasing importance, extent and wealth, large assistance is to be expected in return for the advantages it will derive from its creation."

THE WRECK OF THE "CAROLINE"

CHRISTMAS day, 1836, brought sorrow to the people of Redcar. On that day the Zetland liftboat lost one of its crew. During a heavy north-east gale, the Danish brig *Caroline* was seen running for the beach at Redcar. Caught by the breakers beyond the Saltscar rocks, her crew of nine took to their boats. They were all swept away before the lifeboat could reach them. The crew of the Zetland battled on, rowing through mountainous seas, seeking survivors. As he was preparing to rescue one of the Danish sailors, William Guy was caught by a wave and swept overboard. He was the first and last lifeboat-man to be lost from the Zetland. All the Danish crew perished.

CHAPTER THREE — THE 1840's

BETWEEN 1820 and 1840 there were few changes in the two communities of Redcar and Coatham. Redcar continued to grow steadily; Coatham remained virtually static.

TOTAL POPULATION FIGURES

	Redcar	Coatham
1821	673	686
1831	729	663
1841	794	714

N.B. The Coatham Census figures include the whole of the Parish of Kirkleatham, but they reflect accurately the changes in the resort.

Redcar was still a quiet, select watering place. Its chief attraction was the beach with the broad expanse of firm, smooth sand. There were paddle steamer trips to Newcastle, Tynemouth, Sunderland, Hartlepool, Whitby and Scarborough. Country drives round the district lead the visitor to Wilton, Upleatham, Kirkleatham, Skelton, Guisborough and Ormesby. The following report of the summer season at Redcar is taken from the *Cleveland Repertory and Stokesley Advertiser* of August, 1843:

"We were glad to observe that the fashionable watering place continues crowded with highly respectable families . . . All the lodging houses, and especially those of superior description, have been pretty full during the season, and the principal inns have had far above average patronage, although Mrs. Sowray's has stood first on the list." Mrs. Sowray kept the Red Lion Inn.

White's Directory of 1840 lists eighteen lodging houses at Redcar and there would be many more people who took in occasional paying guests.

There were no lodgings listed for Coatham in that year; the public hotel, where Hutton had stayed thirty years earlier, had become a farmhouse. Writing in 1841, Walbran states in his *Visitor's Guide to Redcar*:

"Now, visitors no longer come to Coatham. The village seems much neglected. Only a few individuals who cannot find accommodation in Redcar, or who prefer privacy and seclusion are to be found there during the bathing season. The bathing machines, so much in use there, have vanished and seem to have joined their rivals at Redcar".

FISHING

In the second edition of his Guide in 1848, Walbran gives details of the fishing industry at Redcar. The fishing grounds were reckoned to extend about twenty miles out to sea but in winter the fishermen rarely ventured more than five miles from the shore. There were about thirty-six cobles at Redcar and they were manned by about one hundred men and boys. The larger cobles were crewed by five men and were forty-six feet long; the cost of the boats varied between £30 and £40. The ordinary cobles were twenty-six feet long and generally rowed by three men. They were built at Hartlepool for between twelve and fifteen guineas. In the past, three men would share the cost of the boat, but, according to Walbran, most fishermen owned their own boats by the 1840's.

Fish were usually sold on the beach as the boats came in. The primitive dialect and the cunning manner in which the bargains were conducted often afforded some amusement to visitors. The fish was chiefly sent to West Riding towns. After the arrival of the railways Redcar fish found its way to Manchester, Birmingham, Nottingham and even to London. Besides the fishing cobles, there were fifteen or sixteen boats used by the pilots to guide vessels to Stockton, Middlesbrough and Hartlepool. Coatham, which had once rivalled Redcar had no cobles at this time; its fishing industry having merged with that of Redcar.

A small salmon fishery flourished in Coatham Bay and the Tees estuary. It was founded by a family called Gaunt in 1830. Their tombstone in Kirkleatham churchyard (north of the church) records their activities. The fish were caught in long nets stretched out into the sea. A separate small industry was the trapping of wild ducks. They were caught in decoy nets on Coatham Marshes (now almost covered by the new steel complex at Redcar).

An officer and six men of the Preventive Service were stationed at Coatham. They had a small armoury at the west end of the village. Walbran had too high an opinion of the neighbourhood "to believe that it is ever required". The days of smuggling had long since passed. Only the oldest people in the village could recall days when smuggled gin was sold relatively openly at a penny a glass.

THE COMING OF THE RAILWAY

THE idea of extending the railway line from Middlesbrough to Redcar was first proposed at a public meeting in the Crown and Anchor. The advantages to the town would be immense. If Redcar was to retain its importance as a resort, the railway was a necessity. Without the railway, Redcar would almost certainly lose its holiday trade to Seaton, Hartlepool and other bathing places. There was even a slight suggestion that the town had already lost a little of its former prosperity. The railway would do much to make the town more accessible; visitors from the south and west of Yorkshire would reach Redcar in under five hours travelling time, it was claimed. Rail transport would be a quicker means of carrying the fish to the great industrial towns of the West Riding where there was already a considerable market for Redcar's produce. A further argument put forward by the proposers was the same as used by the canal builders a century earlier—cheap fuel. Coal cost ten shillings (50p) per ton in Middlesbrough but it cost a further seven shillings and sixpence (37½p) to transport it to Redcar. The cost of transport by rail would be only two shillings per ton. As well as visitors in the bathing season, the railway would furnish cheap transport for all the general and commercial needs of the town.

An Act for extending the line was passed by Parliament in 1845. Work commenced promptly and the line was completed in eight months. The line had only two intermediate stations, between Middlesbrough and Redcar, at Cleveland Port and Lazenby Station (Warrenby Halt). From Middlesbrough the line stayed within sight of the Tees and passed north of Coatham Marshes, the sandbanks offering better foundations. From Marsh House Farm, at Warrenby, the line headed due east to an impressive terminal station in Redcar. The course of the line can still be easily traced along a deep gully running the length of the Cleveland Golf Course, thence along Queen Street. The station was situated precisely where Craigton House now stands at the junction of Queen Street and West Terrace.

The opening was a grand occasion. On June 8th, 1846, the procession left Darlington. Leading the cavalcade was George Stephenson's "Locomotion" which pulled fourteen trucks of coal and lime. Immediately behind was engine "A" of the Great North Eastern Company, pulling a passenger train of twenty carriages. Both engines carried the Union Jack. At Middlesbrough docks all the ships were decked out with flags. Large crowds were gathered all along the route, cheering and waving banners. The momentous journey took two hours.

As Redcar was developing, the neighbouring resort of Saltburn was being discovered. The directors and owners of the iron mines and iron and steel making companies sought pleasant resorts close to their industrial centres, both Redcar and Saltburn fulfilled those needs, as to a lesser extent did Marske-by-the-Sea. Within 15 years, the railway line was extended to Saltburn. West of Coatham, the line was diverted southwards and ran round the south side of Redcar. A new station opened with the line in 1861 and the old was left at the end of a spur. It stood empty for some while and was sold in 1873 as the Central Hall. A market was held inside. Alexander Coverdale leased much of the frontage facing the High Street and Queen Street. A man of divers interests, Coverdale ran a drapers, a gift shop, a jewellers and watchmakers, a circulating library and a printers and stationers.

Towards the end of the century, part of the old station was made into a theatre and in August 1893 or 1894 the D'Oyly Carte Company performed *The Mikado*, on stage. Later the hall was turned into two cinemas, the Central and the Regent. The former was destroyed by fire in 1948 and re-opened in 1954. Pantomime and variety shows were occasionally still performed at the Regent Cinema until the building was demolished in 1964, and the Craigton House development superseded it.

THE WRECK OF THE " SUSANNAH "

IN 1841, the collier brig *Susannah* of Stockton was wrecked off the shore at Coatham. A large crowd was assembled to watch the rescue attempts. Before the lifeboat *Zetland* could reach them, the crew of nine were lost. Eleven other vessels came ashore near the same place in that storm, two were broken up, the remainder refloated.

CHAPTER FOUR — THE 1850's

THE railway extension to Saltburn had not been started so the line shown on the map is the original route from Middlesbrough, via Queen Street to Central Hall. About a mile outside Coatham was Upleatham Junction. A narrow gauge track ran up to the ironstone mines at Upleatham. It crossed Kirkleatham Lane, then Coatham Lane, under Red Bridge—Coatham Bridge; turning south, the track ran alongside Ramshaw's Lane or Low Farm Lane, now Mersey Road. Turning east the line came to West Dike Lane where it swung sharply south again. Turning east again, the route passed a stationary engine, there to assist the passage of loaded trucks up the incline after passing under Redcar Lane. Thence the line turned south-east towards the hills. The line to Saltburn was to follow much the same path and in places to use the same foundations. The low state to which Coatham's popularity as a resort had sunk can be gauged by the routing of the original line between the village and the sea and the extent to which the sidings spread over East Coatham.

Had it not been for the railway, Redcar would still have been a rather isolated place. The town could still be reached only from the south, via Redcar Lane. West Dike Lane was but a track. To the east there was a bridle path along the sandbanks and cliff-tops to Marske. Back Lane ran along the rear of the properties on the south side of Redcar High Street; crossing Redcar Lane it continued towards Coatham, running parallel to and south of Coatham High Street. This is now one of the main through routes across Redcar from west to east—Coatham Road, Milbank Terrace and Lord Street. In 1853 it ended at Coatham Lane, there being nothing but sandbanks and a rabbit warren beyond it. Warrenby was not built until twenty years later.

Coatham was reached along Kirkleatham Lane, then Coatham Lane, from the south. West Coatham Lane ran south of the marshes to outlying farms. This is now Broadway, Dormanstown.

Coatham marshes have seen much history. The Romans camped there, maintaining their chain of signal beacons; signals from Huntcliff beacon could be received and transmitted north towards Hadrian's Wall. The marshes were worked through ancient times to produce salt, traces of these old salt workings can still be seen, although soon they will be lost for ever beneath the relentless spread of the Redcar Works of the British Steel Corporation. There

36

ORDNANCE SURVEY 1855, Published 1857
Part of 1 : 10,560 Sheet, Yorks., N. Riding Sheet 7.
Reduced in size from original scale.

was a regular trade in salt from Coatham to Guisborough Priory and thence to Whitby from the 12th to 15th centuries. In those days Kirkleatham was a flourishing community with several inns and much activity concerned with the passage of trade from the coast inland and along the main coastal road from Yarm towards Whitby.

The original Ordnance Sheet was surveyed in 1855 and published in 1857. The basic scale was six inches to the mile (1 : 10560); there is insufficient detail to permit many particular buildings to be recognised. The census returns of 1851 offer more help.

CENSUS OF 1851

FULL names, exact ages, the relationship of each member of the household to its head, and the sex, occupation and birthplace of each person are all enumerated in the census. Thus an accurate picture of the community can be built up.

Half the people who lived in Redcar were born and bred there. A further thirty per cent came from towns and villages in the North Riding of Yorkshire. Of the remainder, most came from County Durham. More people came to Redcar from Guisborough than any other single place. This obviously arose from the age-old links between the two places. From earliest times fish from Redcar had been sold at Guisborough Market and salt from Coatham had started its journey inland along the same paths. Quite a number of people came from Stockton, another market town and a thriving port.

The census returns for Coatham present a similar picture. Forty per cent were born and bred Coathamians. The highest number of "off-comers" might have been made up partly of immigrant workers who had arrived with the railway and partly from visitors who had settled there when the village had been a popular spa forty years earlier. Most of the 'new' residents had come from towns and villages within twenty-five miles. Many were farmers and agricultural workers. It appears that there was more mobility of labour in the countryside than is generally supposed to have been the case. Of those not born in Yorkshire, most came from the fringes of County Durham—from Stockton, Darlington, Norton, Aycliffe and Bishop Auckland.

The occupations of most of the men of Redcar fell into one of three main groups. One fifth of the working men were fishermen and their sons. Almost as many were engaged in the building trade, a sure indication that the town was growing. The other main group comprised shopkeepers, merchants and craftsmen. Farmers and their labourers totalled twelve per cent and pilots, sailors and other seafarers made up a similar percentage of the male working population. Another small but significant group was that of those living from private income, usually land or house owners. The remaining group included male servants, grooms and coachmen. There were also a surgeon, two schoolmasters, a magistrate, a surveyor and several clergymen. Once built, the railway gave employment to only a small number of men.

Married women did not go out to work. Once married they became housewives, therefore the working female population was almost exclusively women without a man to support them. A large percentage of the widows and spinsters lived from private income; some were annuitants and fund-holders. Others owned property or land. In Redcar, many widows made a living as lodging house keepers. Most of the working women were employed in domestic service; they tended to be young, unmarried and "lived-in". Dressmakers, seamstresses and milliners formed the next most numerous group and a few women worked as laundresses.

Coatham was a very different picture. At the time of the census it was predominantly a farming community; well over one-third of the men worked on the land. The only other sizeable group was that of the shopkeepers and craftsmen. Surprisingly there are no fishermen recorded at Coatham other than the eight salmon fishers. Few women worked at all. Of those who did, most were dressmakers, and they were only thirteen in number. A small number of unmarried girls had come to Coatham to work as domestic servants mainly in the farmhouses.

Primary education was not compulsory at the time, nor was it free. Therefore, nationally, the majority of children did not attend school. The reverse was the case at Redcar where eight out of ten children attended school between the ages of five and twelve years. There were also a few described in the census as "scholars at home" —they had governesses. In only two families in Redcar, both those of fishermen, did the children not receive any formal education. At Coatham, education was free at the village school and all the children who were eligible attended. Consequently there was no recorded child employment, either on farms or in service. At Redcar, three children below the age of twelve were employed; two, aged nine and ten, were errand boys, the other, aged eleven, was in domestic service.

REDCAR

IN the middle of the 19th century, Redcar had become a small town which was beginning to spill over beyond its one main street. Houses had been built behind both sides of the High Street in a rather haphazard fashion. Known as North Side and Back Lane, they grew to become Esplanade and Lord Street. High Street had been steadily growing but had not yet reached its present length; the houses were numbered up one side of the street and down the other. Building was under way at the east end of the High Street as Albion and Clarendon Terraces came into being. At the opposite end was a new hotel; the Railway Hotel had been built diagonally opposite the old station, next to it were two houses known as Railway Terrace. The hotel changed its name to the Clarendon when the old station was closed. Zetland Square, popularly known then, as now, as Fishermen's Square, stood at the eastern extreme of the town. The cause of the nickname was obvious, many fishermen lived there.

The houses in North Side were numbered 1-23 and there were a further half-dozen or so cottages built amongst them. Three side streets were developing between North Side and High Street. Station Street was so named because the old station stood at its corner, later it was renamed West Terrace; it comprised "The Mason's Arms" and one house and the old Zetland School. Bath Street took its name from the bathing establishment of James Carter, situated along the west side of the street and nearest the High Street; there were five other houses in that street. Moore Street, then called Swan Lane had three houses.

Lord Street kept its old title of Back Lane until quite recent times. Eleven houses belonged to the Parish of Upleatham; this was the result of some ancient rights probably concerned with fishing, owned by Upleatham. At least one prospective groom was caught unawares by this anomaly; taking up residence in order to be able to marry a non-resident lady, the young man discovered to his chagrin that he had qualified to be married at Upleatham, not Redcar Church. This detached portion of Upleatham was bounded by the sea to the north, Lord Street to the south, Redcar Lane to the west and stretched east nearly to Zetland Park. West of Redcar Lane, there were ten cottages of which only one had a name; the remainder were addressed simply as "The Cottages, Back Lane". Some of these cottages appear to have been built in the large backyards of High Street houses. This would also have been true of some of the cottages along North Side. Four houses stood in Wellington Place, about halfway along Back Street. Seven terraced houses had been built at the West Dike Lane end of Back Lane; they were known as South Terrace and four still stand. Altogether there were over thirty dwellings in Back Lane.

Church Street was at the bottom of Redcar Lane; there were twelve houses and a little distance away was the Parsonage. There was also the mill house and Redcar's six-sailed windmill.

COATHAM

THE village had changed little since Hutton's visit. It still had one long street, built only along the south side. The census of 1851 listed seventy-five houses along Coatham High Street, Marsh House (farm) and four houses nearby, making a total of eighty. The same figure as Hutton had estimated in 1810. Development was in its infancy in the mid-nineteenth century. The first new houses were in Victoria Terrace, now part of Coatham Road.

Many of these old names are still to be found around the town. They are preserved on plaques, some quite ornate, high on the fronts of the terraces. Look for them near the centre or at the ends just below the eaves. In Station Road you can find Newcomen Street; Queen Street has King James Terrace; Dundas Place was nearly obscured by the fascia of W. H. Smith's shop in the High Street; Hobson's Terrace is on West Dyke Road. There are many more to be found.

The old railway station was occupied by one family. Behind it, in splendid isolation on the sandbanks, roughly on the brow of the hill in Turner Street, stood Railway Terrace. It comprised four white brick houses for railway workers. They were later dismantled and rebuilt at Kirkleatham where they are now preserved by the National Trust.

At the corner of West Dike Lane and Milbank Terrace was The Green House, with a smaller house nearby. Coatham's windmill and mill house stood near to the junction of Station Road and Coatham Road. The United Reformed Church stands precisely on the site of the old windmill. Near the Lobster Inn were several more houses, one of which was the school house. At the corner of Rocket Terrace and High Street was another public house, the "Waterloo Tavern". There was considerable building in the long gardens behind some of the fishermen's cottages.

CHOLERA

REDCAR was no longer a small village. By the 1850's the need for sanitary reform could no longer be ignored. Cholera was the dread of Victorian England. It struck both rich and poor. In over half the cases the disease proved fatal. Death came suddenly, usually within twenty-four hours. Redcar belonged to the Guisborough Poor Law Union. The Medical Officer of Health was much concerned. He foresaw the dangers to health arising from the unsanitary conditions prevalent in the town. The problem was really one of persuasion and enforcement. There was no governing body for the town to pay for the improvements and enforce sanitation laws. He raised the matter of sanitation with the Guardians of the Poor. They ignored his recommendations.

In September, 1854, cholera broke out. There were twenty cases and eight deaths in the town. Seven of the deaths occurred in Fishermen's Square, which was described in the contemporary press as a very dirty and ill-ventilated place. The owner of the property was the Earl of Zetland.

The Earl of Zetland took immediate and drastic action. He ordered the whole of the square to be pulled down and replaced with an entirely new street for the fishermen. It was a row of twenty-two terraced houses built "with every sanitary improvement calculated to prevent the recurrence of the disease". The row was directly to the south of the original square and called South Terrace. Today it bears the same name but it is still more popularly known as "Fishermen's Square". In the centre of the row is a lookout position from which a watch could be kept for fishing boats returning and in times of storm for vessels in distress. Behind the terrace is a row of bait-houses where nets and tackle would be stored and maintained. There are still several fishing families in residence.

The action of the Guardians of the Poor was typically English. They formed a committee. This body met to inspect the nuisances at Redcar. A month later a Sanitary Committee was appointed. Its members were dutiful and known members of the community but it is difficult to determine what improvements they effected.

Typhus followed the cholera within weeks. The epidemic was confined to the poorer parts of the town. There were thirty cases in Back Lane with one fatality. There were two more deaths on North Side. The outbreak appears to have stemmed from Smith Street, a newly-built block at the east end of Back Street. In December, 1854, a petition was forwarded to the General Board of Health asking that the provisions of the Public Health Acts be applied to the town. The General Board sent Inspector Ranger to report on the conditions locally.

The report, made in 1855, shows how the insanitary state of the town led to the outbreak of disease. The Ranger Report makes fascinating reading. It shows Redcar as a rather smelly dirty place; not quite up to the idealistic pictures of the town drawn in the early guides and directories.

In the bathing season, water was obtained from a spring three and a half miles from the town. It was sold to visitors and the wealthier residents at the rate of a halfpenny a gallon. The majority of the residents were dependent on wells for their supply. These tended to be shallow—between four and sixteen feet—and often adjacent to cesspools. There were many instances of wells being infused with seepage from the cesspools. In one case the seepage was such that the water had to be filtered before use. For inhabitants without wells of their own, there was a public pump.

The town was without drains and sewers, except for those

leading to cesspools or ashpits. Those houses with water closets drained into the cesspools and the foul contents were allowed to escape and seep away as best as nature could provide. The cesspits behind the houses on North Side were in the sandbanks and only a few feet from the dwellings. On the south side of the town, the roadside gutters led the sewage to open ditches. It was then left to stagnate in the fields. A local builder stated at the time that the soil had become "putrid, foul and offensive and had been the great cause of sickness. Unless something is done to remedy the existing evils, the town will be ruined". Although water closets were found in the lodging houses, the usual convenience was the ash pit privy in an outhouse at the end of the backyard to each house. At one time in Fishermen's Square, one privy served ninety-five people. Hence the force with which cholera had struck. The last signs of the outdoor privies can be seen at the rear of Queen Street. Low in the walls are wooden frames, about two feet square, which formerly contained doors; now they are bricked up. The doors hinged at the bottom and the top swung outwards. Hanging on the inside of the door was a receptacle; with the door closed the bin would be positioned beneath the seat. Night soil was removed regularly.

When Ranger made his report, there was no scavenger, as the privy emptier was called. The responsibility for emptying the ash pits lay with the occupiers of the property. A responsibility to which they did not take kindly, or attend to frequently. Refuse was thrown into the road, or the open gutters, or even simply left to accumulate. The Medical Officer of Health considered these accumulations a further source of disease.

During the previous decade, houses had been built quickly to accommodate the rapidly increasing population. The development was not fettered by building regulations and not checked by health authorities. Houses could and were erected with no regard for public health. Smith Street, source of the typhus, was a prime example, being a block of eight houses built back-to-back. Another block of back-to-back houses was Lynas Place, condemned in 1924 and still standing in 1980. Small houses were being crowded into the yards and courts behind the High Street. Some of these can still be seen from the Esplanade and Lord Street. Then there was the original Fishermen's Square. The MOH attributed the cholera outbreak to "the very wretched principles on which the cottages had been built".

Inspector Ranger recommended that the Public Health Acts be applied to Redcar forthwith. This gave the ratepayers the right to elect a Local Board of Health which would be responsible for carrying out the necessary improvements in the town. The problems were not restricted to Redcar. A few miles away, the townships of Eston, South Bank and Normanby were enduring similar tribulations as they exploded into being with the arrival of the iron and steel industries. These Local Boards were the forerunners of the modern Councils.

REDCAR LOCAL BOARD OF HEALTH

IN June, 1855, a year after the typhus and cholera, the Redcar Local Board of Health was formed and modern Redcar began to take shape. The first problems to be tackled were, of course, those of drainage and sewerage. Next on the list was to be the provision of a good water supply—to be furnished from a reservoir to be built at Upleatham. The first of the Board's Minute Books covering 1855-60 is missing, the remainder are kept at the Cleveland County Archivist Office. The surveyor's letter book of that early period describes the situation.

The drainage of the town was completed within two years. The Board installed the main drains and each householder was required to pay for private drains to be connected to the system. One old lady who refused to comply with the regulations had the drains installed by the Board which then compelled her to pay for the work. Once the main drainage work was completed, it fell to the surveyor to investigate and deal with complaints of nuisance. There were several complaints about dung heaps in back yards and pig sties; one cesspool was described as "full of filth . . . and stunk awfully". Having endured a generation of squalid conditions, it required considerable effort to bring the poorer areas in line with the basic standards; there were reports of great quantities of slops and soap suds being thrown daily into the gutters of Back Lane, such that a special statute was called for, to restrict the practice.

The next improvement came in 1857 with the introduction of gas lighting. The first place to be illuminated was St. Peter's Parish Church. Then many of the business premises were lit up and a week later the street lights were lit. The gas was provided under a contract with the Redcar Gas Company. There seems to have been a certain status attached to having a gas lamp outside one's premises. There were many letters exchanged later in the century regarding the location of a lamp at the junction of West Dyke Road with Milbank Terrace and Lord Street; the church elders felt it would be of greatest use outside the Congregational Church; the landlord of the Royal Standard and the residents of the Green House all had similar views regarding their corner of the junction.

THE ZETLAND SCHOOL

THE present Zetland School was built at the expense of the second Earl of Zetland in 1859, and the scholars were transferred from the old school in West Terrace. The new building had a hall, a classroom and a house for the headmaster. It was attended by one hundred and thirty children. The school was examined annually by an inspector. In 1863 the inspector pronounced it to be the best in his district; the reports were forwarded to the Earl of Zetland. The close relations between the school and the church are indicated by the entries in the School Log Books which date from 1863.

> "Examination this afternoon in scripture . . . the Vicar of Coatham conducted it in the presence of a great number of ladies and gentlemen of the neighbourhood."

Questions would include many things learned by rote, including the Ten Commandments, the Catechism, Creed and Lord's Prayer. Quite an ordeal for the children.

The headmaster's entries in the Log Books reflect the social changes occurring throughout the town. There are frequent references to the "season". School attendance would fall considerably during the summer as the older girls were kept at home to help with housework. Succinctly, the headmaster wrote: "The girls are beginning to drop off, my 'summer' is passed and the town's is commencing." On another occasion he wrote: "Redcar is filling fast with visitors and the shopkeepers are getting every available boy to run errands. Several are driving donkeys and fully half of the girls are at home." In later years, Redcar Races proved to be another distracting magnet for the children; there were also the Regatta and Fair Days. With perhaps a touch of despair, the Log Book notes: "There was never such a place as Redcar for disturbing influences on attendance in summer-time".

Many entries refer to the shipwrecks which inevitably meant low attendance figures, either to watch the disaster as it occurred or to comb the beaches afterwards for jetsam. An entry in January, 1866 is typical: "Three ships ashore . . . half the school absent." The heavy deposits of sea-coal on the beach following a storm also diverted the energies of the children, as they helped their parents gather this free fuel. Sickness and disease still spread easily through the community despite the improved sanitary conditions. In 1870 the headmaster wrote: "Smallpox is proving very fatal among the children, four dying this week." Attendance was so low and the risk of infection so high throughout the town that the school was eventually closed for a month. The school was closed again in 1884 on the advice of the Medical Officer of Health, when scarlet fever raged through the town. The one direct reference to the Ironworks in the district comes in 1878, when the headmaster explains the fall in the number of pupils on the roll. Because of a depression in the iron trade, the population had contracted and many families had suffered very great distress during the previous hard winter.

School fees continued to be paid at the National Schools until late in the century. Free education commenced in 1891, but parents still paid sixpence (2½p) per quarter. Not until 1898 did education become entirely free.

In 1889, Her Majesty's Inspector of Schools reported that the accommodation at the school was insufficient for the size of the parish. Lord Zetland promptly came to the rescue and had the school considerably enlarged. Zetland School was maintained by the Zetlands until it was taken over by the North Riding County Council in 1904.

CHAPTER FIVE — THE 1860's

THE Plan of Redcar, 1861, was originally published as *Peat's Plan*, an advertisement for the chemist of that name, trading in the High Street, and appeared as a supplement to the *Redcar and Saltburn Gazette*. It was intended as a guide to visitors, with hotels and lodging houses marked along with several other places which would be of interest to the visitor. Mr. Peat's premises were in the High Street where Marks and Spencers now stands.

During the 1850's, a number of short terraces had been added to the existing streets. At the east end of the High Street, Albion and Clarendon Terraces had been completed and Granville Terrace laid out. At the west end, were North Terrace and Dundas Place. Marine Terrace, on the sea front, was to become part of the Esplanade. Portland Terrace in West Dike Lane and South Terrace in Lord Street had been built; by 1861 Back Lane had changed its name to that which we now know. Development was beginning to move out from the High Street; Albert Street was under construction and Alma Parade was being laid out. Most of the main streams of Christian beliefs had arrived. The plan shows that in addition to St. Peter's Parish Church, there were Congregational, Wesleyan and Primitive Methodist Chapels and a Friends' Meeting House.

Bathing was still an important activity. The nineteenth century fostered the creation of many special health resorts. Redcar joined the ranks of health spas by offering the 'medicinal' qualities of sea water. Dr. Horner's Hydropathic Establishment, near the Royal Hotel on the Esplanade was believed to be the only one in Great Britain using cold salt water to "cure all ills". Conventional hot or cold showers, or baths were available at the two other bath houses. The newsroom, with its daily newspapers, appears to have been roughly in the same place as Redcar's original thatched Post Office. For those who preferred indoor pastimes, the Red Lion, The Royal and the Zetland Rooms (later the Zetland Hotel) offered billiards.

A VISITOR'S HANDBOOK, 1863

TWEDDEL published his *Visitor's Handbook to Redcar, Coatham and Saltburn by the Sea* in 1863. Redcar had improved somewhat since Hutton visited the village in 1810. The mud-walled dwellings had given way to neatly built cottages (a few remain on the Esplanade between the lifeboat house and the pier ballroom) and handsome lodging houses. The appearance of the High Street had been improved by the removal of the low buildings in front of the old cottages; the mountains of drift sands had also been removed, making travelling less hazardous. "The spring cart of the farmer or tradesman and the chariot of the aristocrat now bowl along the street without the least impediment" notes Tweddel.

The improvements were such as to be rated as newsworthy by the *Middlesbrough News and Cleveland Advertiser*. On July 27th, 1861 there was printed a report entitled *The Sea-Side—A Visit to Redcar*. The streets were no longer paved with sand; there were pavements in all the principal thoroughfares and leading down to the beach. The town was thoroughly drained and was dry and healthy. All this was the work of the Local Board of Health. The only fault the reporter noted was that the outlet of the main sewer was above the low water mark and that at times "unpleasant smells and noxious exhalations" wafted across the beach. Responsibility for cleaning the beach lay with the Local Board of Health. One Mark Baker successfully tendered in 1861 for removing all fish refuse from the sands.

The Local Board was concerned with improving the appearance of the town and particularly with increasing its attractions as a seaside resort. An early scheme was to have the old buildings removed from the middle of the High Street. The first major construction scheme was the building of a sea wall and promenade. Completed in 1869 it ran the full length of the existing town and permitted visitors, and residents, to walk out in all but the worst of weathers. The surveyor was instructed to procure twelve seats to be placed along what we know as the Esplanade; they were to be painted green. Redcar was developing and expanding at a brisk rate and it was apparent that some form of control was needed to enforce reasonable standards. In 1863 a committee was appointed to prepare Building By-Laws and to lay the same before the Local Board for approval.

Despite the improvements, some visitors were still critical. An unknown author, disenchanted with the town, penned the following in 1864 and addressed it to the "Good People of Redcar":

A PARTING WORD, or
REDCAR AS IT IS AND REDCAR AS IT SHOULD BE
"Redcar, the glorious sandy old town of one street, where the houses are as irregular, as unsystematic, as unarchitectural,

as unconformable with each other as the most ingenious, botching house-planner could possibly contrive."

The sea front rated poorly too:

". . . with its zig-zag series of single-decker, higgledy-piggledy, gipsy-like hovels. The discharge pipes . . . whence everything that is disgusting and nauseous is constantly oozing under the very noses of every passer-by. Don't allow the shore to be made a continual muck-heap and you will have visitors in shoals."

The anonymous critic was correct in an assumption made later in his address: the roof line of the cottages on the sea-front had been deliberately kept low so as not to impede the views for the High Street guest houses. Despite the efforts of the Local Board he found the town little improved, although he conceded that the supply of gas and water was beneficial. The benefits of the drainage and sewerage systems he found somewhat negated by the continuing habit of the natives to throw the domestic refuse "in filthy and disgusting rubbish heaps around the houses". After admonishing the residents sternly, he looked to the future.

His plan was quite clear. First, the residents should "pull down every one of those dirty, little one-storeyed excrescences"; in their place should be built a promenade of new terraces of lodging houses, overlooking the sea. The High Street should be reserved exclusively for shops. In addition, he felt that the town needed a market and a park where visitors could stroll would be a fine amenity. He hoped that his address would make the people of Redcar bestir themselves; he felt that they did not appreciate their own town, yet they had much of which to be proud. Although in some matters a full half-century ahead of his time, this critical visitor foresaw quite accurately the form in which the resort was to develop. The massive terraces were built along the sea-front; the discharge pipes were extended much further out to sea; a market was established and survived several sites and variations in popularity until 1956; parks were established.

THREE FAMOUS VISITORS

NATHANIEL HAWTHORNE, an American whose works include *The Scarlet Letter* and *Tanglewood Tales*, stayed in Redcar with his family from July to October, 1859. They arrived by train from Scarborough and spent their first night at the Clarendon Hotel, it being adjacent to the existing railway terminus.

The following day they moved to a lodging house on the corner of King Street and High Street, where they boarded for the remainder of their stay. Hawthorne chose Redcar because he wanted a quiet location whilst working on the final draft of his novel *The Magic Fawn*. The town proved much busier than the family had anticipated. In a letter to her sister, Mrs. Hawthorne said: "We thought this would be out of the way and solitary but were much mistaken. It is, however, not quite so expensive as Whitby, which is more reasonable than Scarborough."

Charles Dickens was unimpressed by Redcar in 1844 and described it as a "long cell". The story goes that he walked down to the beach. With carpet-bag in hand he cast one mournful glance at Coatham, another at Redcar, turned on his heel and walked away. He was travelling towards Whitby and had elected to see the coast rather than use the established moorland route. Dickens made his way to Marske where he lodged overnight in the Dundas Arms (adjacent to the roundabout in Marske High Street where there is now a raised terrace of shops). His journey thence was not uncomplicated: the carrier who undertook to transport him to Whitby stayed too long for Dicken's liking enjoying a parade with bands in Loftus.

Samuel Plimsoll resided for a while in a house where Marks and Spencers now have a shop. Walking along the beach he could not fail to observe the "coffin ships". These old sailing vessels were all in poor condition and usually dangerously overloaded, their owners being anxious to carry as high a payload as possible. The boats attracted their nick-name from the frequency with which they foundered and the consequent high loss of lives. Plimsoll observed that the boats sank or rose predictably, as they were loaded or unloaded. As a result of his observations, a line was to be painted round the side of all vessels to indicate the loading capacity. The Plimsoll Line became law in the Merchant Shipping Act of 1876.

THE REVIVAL OF COATHAM

THE *Middlesbrough News and Cleveland Advertiser* reported in June, 1866 on the summer season at Redcar and at Coatham. The latter had not enjoyed a reported "season" for over three decades; that coincidentally was the time that the village was separated from the shore by the early railway line which had run to the old Central Station. By June, the season was well under way at Redcar and there were many visitors in the town. With more accommodation available at new lodging houses, a very busy summer was expected; three or four of the new guest houses were right on the sea front. The newspaper reporter describes the "magnificent houses, four storeys high, with uninterrupted views of the sea at Coatham", presumably Newcomen Terrace. Coatham Road then comprised a series of beautiful terraces and some villas, stretching from Victoria Terrace to Coatham Church, over half a mile away. There are more houses close to the new railway station; in all, accommodation for several hundred more visitors. The contemporary guides and directories again make copious references to the amenities of Coatham, no longer regarding it as a poor adjunct to Redcar.

The community had grown sufficiently to need and support its own church. Christ Church, Coatham was built in 1854 at the expense of Mrs. Newcomen of Kirkleatham Hall; most of the land in Coatham belonged to the Kirkleatham Estate. Mrs. Newcomen also provided the living for the priest and a further sum for repairs as they became necessary. Originally the church was under the care of the vicar of Kirkleatham, it was constituted a separate parish in 1860. Standing in splendid isolation, with the village to its north and Kirkleatham and the Cleveland Hills to the south, the new building soon became known as the "Church-in-the-fields". The beauty of the church impressed many. Tweddel declared it to be "decidedly the most beautiful church in Cleveland". St. Peter's church, Redcar was dismissed as "a poor affair" by the *Middlesbrough News and Advertiser*. The report continued: "Coatham Church is quite the reverse, being a handsome structure with an elegant tower and spire. A century of grime has possibly dulled its beauty somewhat, or perhaps the twentieth century expects greater things ; Sir Nicholas Pevsner describes the same church as "dull . . . though remarkably, all the original stained glass remains intact".

Mrs. Newcomen was also patron of the Reading Room and Library which had a membership of sixty. The good lady also built and maintained a National School in 1866. Ten years later the management of the school came under the Kirkleatham School Board but reverted to the Church Authorities when the Boards were later abolished. Coatham Church of England School remained in use as a school until 1969 when it was replaced by a new building 200 yards away and the old building became a study centre for teachers. In the same year that Mrs. Newcomen founded the National School, the Society of Friends opened their Meeting House in Coatham.

Coatham's most famous school was Sir William Turner's Grammar School; one hundred boys, including twenty boarders were taught there. Sir William Turner was a wool trader of considerable standing in the City of London in the seventeenth century. He was President of the Boards of Bridewell and Bethlehem (Bedlam) Hospitals and was Lord Mayor of London in 1669. Having amassed a considerable fortune, Sir William founded in 1676 the almshouses known as Kirkleatham Hospital (rebuilt 1742). On his death in 1692 he bequeathed £3000 to create a free school. With the money, in 1708-9 Cholmley Turner built what is now known as The Old Hall, Kirkleatham. This generous building housed the school; the master lived in and received £100 per year; and the usher £50. In later years, the school was converted to a private house and the education of the children continued in the Hospital, which sheltered ten boys and ten girls, in addition to the score of old men and women. The Charity Commissioners ordered that the school be re-established and what was to be known as Sir William Turner's School was built on Coatham Road in 1869, where Redcar Central Library is now placed. (This building was replaced a century later when Sir William Turner's Grammar School was opened on Corporation Road, now Saltscar School. The name is preserved in Sir William Turner's 6th Form College on Redcar Lane).

The school built in 1869 was large and impressive. The east end first floor contained a chapel with a rose window. Below this room was the scholars' entrance and cloakroom. The central portion of the ground floor contained the large dining room behind an attractive colonnade; next to it was the kitchen with a huge fireplace. Above the dining room was a large library. The west end of the building provided living quarters for the headmaster and his domestic staff. Classrooms were above the library.

COATHAM CONVALESCENT HOME

REVEREND John Postlethwaite, first vicar of Christ Church, Coatham, bought a parcel of land from Mrs. Newcomen in 1860. On it he built and furnished Coatham Convalescent Home. The Home was opened on 22nd May, 1861. It was a red brick edifice with courses of decorative blue and white bricks and was situated near the junction of Queen Street and Newcomen Terrace. There were magnificent views across Coatham Bay towards Hartlepool. The steady flow of sailing vessels into the Tees and along the coast would help the inmates of the Home pass the time. When opened, fifty patients were accommodated and they were tended by voluntary workers. Later the Home was extended and a chapel built. A further wing was added to cater for mothers with their children; the Home became known as the Coatham Convalescent Home and Children's Hospital.

The patients were 'poor and respectable persons' recovering from sickness and requiring a change of air and sea bathing, mainly miners from County Durham. Subscribers and donors recommended patients for admission. A donation of five guineas entitled the donor to make one recommendation in that year; ten guineas, two recommendations and so forth. Annual subscribers could send one patient for every two guineas. The usual term of residence was one month, although this could be extended if thought necessary. Medical attention, board and lodge, washing and baths, and everything essential to the health and comfort of the patients were provided free of charge. Although founded by an Anglican priest, patients of all religious denominations were admitted; the only condition being that they attended morning and evening prayers conducted by the Church of England Chaplain. All the nurses and attendants worked on a voluntary basis, receiving no payment at all. The nurses were known as Sisters of the Home of the Good Samaritan; however, they were not necessarily members of a recognised Holy Order.

The Convalescent Home served its original function until shortly before the Second World War. During that war, troops were billeted there. After the war, Redcar Borough Council bought the property and in 1951 the home was demolished. A decade later, the **Coatham Bowl** was built to house an American-style ten-pin bowling alley. It is now a leisure centre.

Coatham Marshes, 1976   Plate 1

Nov.r 1812.

Subscribers to the Hearse, Built for the use of the Townships of Redcar, Marsh and Upleatham. — This is a Copy of the original Put up in Marsh Church on Sat.y the 9.th Day of Jan.y 1813 —————————— by P.Walton Off.r Station'd at Red..

	£. s. d.
R.t Hon.ble Lord Dundas - - - - - - - - -	5„ 0„ 0
Hon.ble Lawrence Dundas Esq.r M.P. - - - - - -	2„ 0„ 0
Jonathan Millner - - - - - - - - - - -	1„ 0„ 0

Subscribers to the Hearse

(a Copy fr.m y.e oldbook)
—————— Regulation Relative to the hire of the Hearse When wanted by those who are not Subscribers, viz:

	s. d.
From Redcar to — Marsh Church — —	2„ 6
To Stokesley or near to it - - - - - - - - - -	10„ 6
To Guisb.o - - - - - - - - - - - - - - -	6„ 0
To Ormesby - - - - - - - - - - - - - - -	6„ 0
To Wilton - - - - - - - - - - - - - - -	4„ 0
To Kirkleatham - - - - - - - - - - - - -	3„ 0
To Skelton - - - - - - - - - - - - - -	5„ 0

N.B: The Hearse is not to go further than 20 miles fr.m Redcar; and the Innkeep.r who takes her away is to make the charge as above for the use of her, (to those that Employ them) and they are to be accountable for the same to the Minister of Marsh. — and all Cash so Rec.d by said Minister is to be kept for Repairs &.c of said Hearse & y.e House she is kept in, and + also to help to Purchase a new Clock when wanted, Witness W.m Millette & J.n Harrison, Minister of Marsh.

Hearse Regulations and Fees

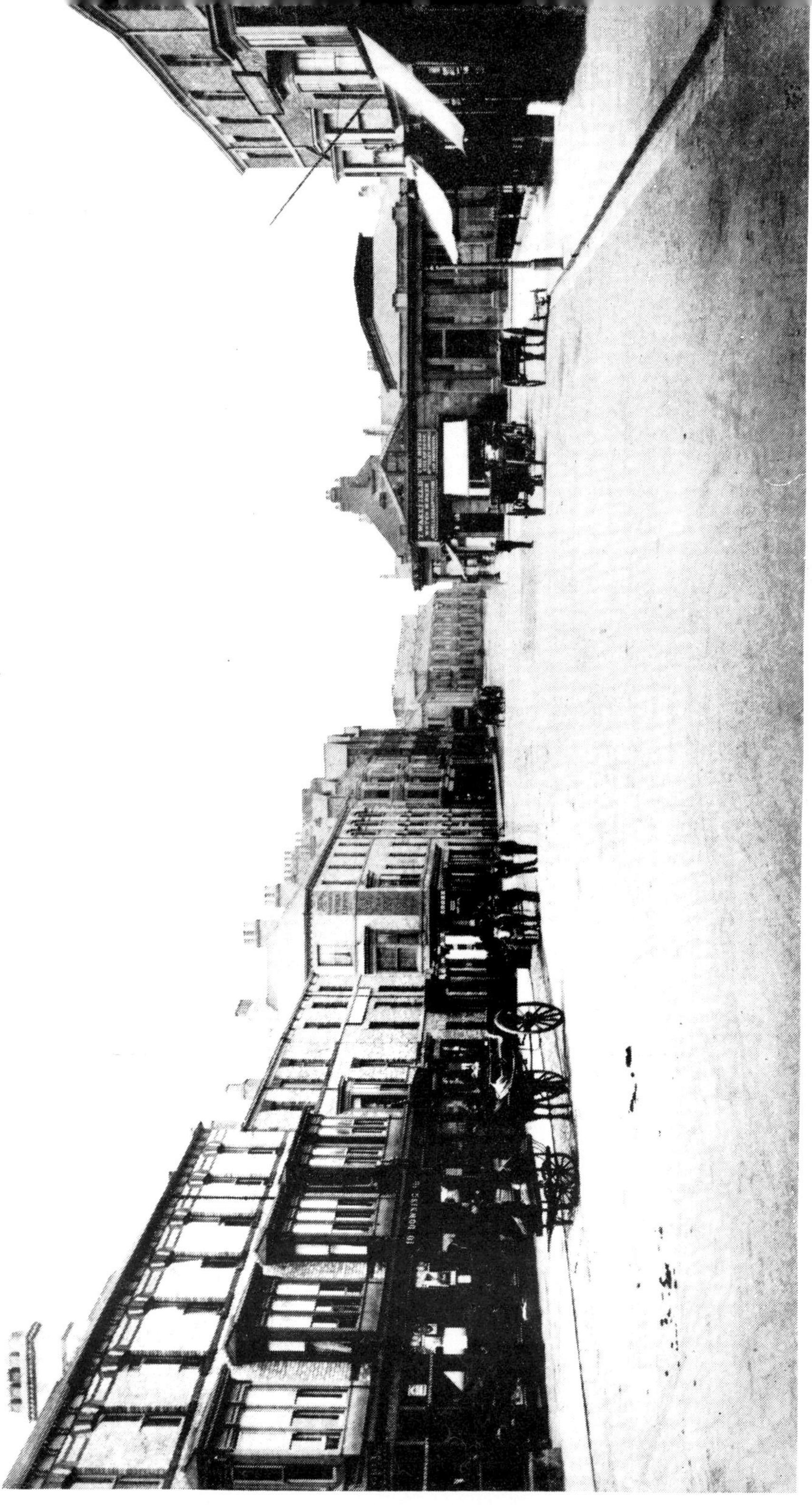

The Oldest Lifeboat in the World. The "Zetland" of Redcar.

Plate 4

Esplanade and Newcomen Terrace, 1890

Plate 5

Esplanade, 1890

Marsh House Farm, Warrenby, 1926

Plate 6

Coronation Gift — a Tin of Toffees

The Steam Roundabout on the Beach, 1904

Plate 7

Spence's Victoria Baths, Coatham, 1884

Plate 8

CHAPTER SIX — 1870 - 1875

BEFORE the census of 1871, the Registrar General had suggested that in streets with two sides the houses should be re-numbered, one side having odd numbers and the other the even numbers. In December, 1870, the whole of the Redcar Local Board of Health met as a special committee to consider the re-numbering of property and the naming of streets within its jurisdiction. One small problem concerned that part of the town which still was under the control of Upleatham Parish; that part of the High Street kept its old numbers and the Upleatham portions of the Esplanade and Lord Street remained un-numbered. The High Street had more or less reached its present length by 1871. There were four new hotels, the Queen, the Globe, the Zetland and the Prince of Wales; none of which remain today.

Along the Esplanade there were more than twice as many houses as had been recorded in the 1851 census. Some re-numbering had taken place and there were a number of cottages still known only by their name. There were seven houses in Lynas Place and six in Pybus Place. These thirteen houses were undoubtedly the darkest blemish on Redcar's sunny countenance; built back-to-back, they were crammed into a space off the Esplanade, access was along a dark passage one metre wide. Even the Local Board's earliest building Bye-Laws prohibited such conditions; the houses had been built immediately prior to the enactment of the Bye-laws. The side-streets joining the High Street to the Esplanade were all in existence by 1871. Dundas Street ran where previously Pounder's Baths had stood. Three other new streets had been named; King Street, Graffenburg Street and Clarendon Street.

Lord Street appears to have been developed still on the north side only, apart from one or two terraces at its west end, as it had not been re-numbered. Many dwellings had been built in the large yards behind the premises on the south side of the High Street. There were six such yards, each with several houses or cottages. Unlike similar courts in other towns, the yards were not overcrowded, but the houses were very small and meanly constructed. Guy's Yard was the largest, with five houses. Many of these buildings still stand, now used mainly as store rooms or outhouses by the adjacent High Street properties; Two of these rough and ready buildings can be seen in Potts Yard at the rear of 118 High Street. (Remember that such places are private property and there is no public right of access).

Since the railway line had been extended to Saltburn and moved south, the land between the new line and Lord Street had started to be filled in with small squares and terraces. After Albert Street and Alma Parade on *Peat's Plan of Redcar*, came ten cottages in Wilton Street and two in Cleveland Street. Three houses known as West End filled the gap between the Clarendon and the Royal Standard Hotels; the beginning of West Dyke Road as we know it. Beyond the railway line lay only the gas works and gas house.

The growth of Redcar during the two decades prior to 1871 seems insignificant when compared with the explosion of development at Coatham. The small agricultural village had become virtually a new town. Unlike Redcar, the growth did not evolve from the old main street; new streets and terraces had been laid out, to a recognisable plan, across the common land which had separated the two communities.

The main development had taken place along what is now Coatham Road. It was made up of several individually named terraces, Milbank, Victoria, Cleveland, Portland, Marine, Bentinck and Vansittart. Amongst these new rows there were a number of villas and large cottages including the following: Clyde, Stanley and Wiltshire cottages and Grant, Clifford and Poona villas. On the south side of Coatham Road between the Grammar School and the cricket field stood Coatham Villas. These were the largest houses in Coatham, with long walled gardens to their south and with vegetable gardens beyond. Those that remain are now all public buildings. Those demolished have been replaced by a public library, a health centre, and a hotel. The largest of all the Coatham Villas is now an office of Langbaurgh Borough Council; earlier in its life it housed Redcar Borough Council. When these magnificently appointed homes were built they were for the wealthiest members of the community: Redcar was a popular dormitory for the families of the iron magnates of Middlesbrough and the south bank of the Tees.

The two terraces overlooking the cricket field merit special mention. This style of architecture was quite new to the district. Both terraces are almost perfectly symmetrical; Nelson Terrace has at each end a hexagonal turret with a spire. Opposite, Trafalgar Terrace is cement rendered and painted, instead of being white and decorated bricks, and has a dominating dormer gable in its centre.

Undoubtedly the finest home in Coatham, at that time, was "Red Barns". Built for the ironmaster, Thomas Hugh Bell, it was here that Gertude Lowthian Bell spent her childhood. A plaque on the north wall records simply that she was a "scholar, administrator and peacemaker. A friend of Arabs". The first woman to graduate from Oxford with a first in modern history, Gertrude Bell moved into diplomatic circles and fell in love with her "beloved east". Wherever she travelled, her notebook and camera went too. Regions hitherto unreached by Europeans were visited, surveyed and explored. Turning to archaeology, she established the National Museum of Baghdad. English to the end, Gertrude Bell dressed in European fashions; yet to the Arabs she was a great sheikh. At her funeral were great numbers of Arabs; their tribute—"If this is a woman, what must the men be like".

For half a century until 1977, 'Red Barns' was the house where the boarders of Sir William Turner's school lived. Many past headmasters and families lived there too.

The middle strata of houses is represented by Newcomen Street, now Station Road; the houses were small enough to make impressive homes, yet large enough to be used as small guest houses.

Alongside the ostentatious houses, the humbler dwellings were growing in number. Pierson's Buildings stood near the junction of Ridley Street and Kirkleatham Street; these were twelve cottages, probably for labourers or agricultural workers. Pierson Street stretched for some length, discreetly behind the smart terraces of Coatham Road. In 1871 it was essentially a row of miners' cottages. Coatham High Street was linked to Coatham Road by Lobster Terrace; apart from these five houses, the old High Street seems to have stood apart from its new neighbours. It appears to have changed little in a score of years; there was the same number of dwellings as in the census of 1851. These were the homes of the local craftsmen and agricultural labourers; all that remained of the old village community of Coatham.

THE CENSUS OF 1871

IN twenty years, the population of Redcar had doubled. That of Coatham had more than trebled.

TOTAL POPULATION FIGURES

	Redcar	Coatham
1851	1032	456
1871	1943	1553

A new group of workers appeared in the census figures for the first time. With the discovery of ironstone in the Cleveland Hills, miners from all over the country had headed for the district. Every village and town within easy reach of the hills above Eston and Marske had a dramatic influx of newcomers. Whole new towns were created: New Marske, Eston, Grangetown, South Bank, all stretched along the south bank of the Tees and served the mining and iron-making communities. Over half of the miners who settled in Redcar were born outside the county; most came from Norfolk, Lincolnshire and Gloucestershire. This was the era of agricultural depression and falling wages for farmworkers. Many left the land to find richer pickings in industry. Many more of the newcomers were shopkeepers and craftsmen and tradesmen. This group made up one-fifth of the male working population. As in the earlier census, the next largest group were building workers. Despite the dramatic growth in the town, the number of fishermen remained static and in 1871 they were ten per cent of the working population. With the extension of the railway, the number of people employed by the railway company had risen, gate-keepers, pointsmen, plate-layers and several porters lived in the town. New professions to the town included a photographer and a jet manufacturer. Redcar had become a town of shopkeepers and lodging house keepers. Those who worked with their hands tended to be employed beyond the town boundaries. Domestic service was still the main occupation for the women of the town. There were still more situations than ever for domestic servants, needed to tend the middle class occupiers of the new terraced houses and villas.

The structure of Coatham was more complex. With its return to public favour in preference to Redcar, the large comfortable houses catered more for professional people and "white-collar" workers. The largest occupational group was again that of the builders. Next came the shopkeepers and tradesmen, although far less in number than their fellows at Redcar. There were a few ironstone miners, half as many as at Redcar. Fewer men worked the land and lived in Coatham. Farmers and their labourers totalled less than eight per cent of the working population; this was probably the most significant change in the structure of Coatham and together with the loss of the fishing community two decades earlier, indicated the path along which the village would grow.

The working class accounted for half the employed population. The remaining half would all fall into a category headed "professional". It was a diverse group of clerks, agents, merchants, and brokers. Coatham had become the residential area for the merchants and industrialists of Middlesbrough amongst whom were to be found several iron-masters, ship-builders, iron-refiners, a brick manufacturer and the owner of a colliery. Thus established, the importance of Coatham and its residents increased steadily for the remainder of the nineteenth century. Although smaller in terms of actual population, Coatham was obviously more prosperous than the neighbouring resort; there were far more domestic servants employed and they tended to be specified as particular posts, such as nurses, cooks or housemaids. Very few Redcar households employed more than one servant, other than the lodging houses.

The arrival of the professional classes to Coatham no doubt raised the prestige of the place. This is reflected in its return to popularity as a resort. To the one lodging-house-keeper of 1851 had been added fifteen more by 1871 (in some instances one establishment was run by two sisters or two widows). Other widowed or unmarried ladies let off parts of their houses as furnished apartments.

THE IRON WORKS

UNTIL the 1870's, Redcar and Coatham had remained outside the area of industrial growth along the banks of the Tees. In 1873 an iron works was established about a mile from Coatham. There were six blast furnaces; the two blast furnaces of Coatham Ironworks, north of the railway line were erected by Messrs. Downey and Company: the four furnaces of the Redcar Works, south of the railway were completed the following year for Messrs. Walker, Maynard and Company. The opening of the ironworks was reported without great enthusiasm in the local newspapers. It was probably considered that the reputations of Redcar and Coatham as resorts would not be enhanced by publishing extensive details of the new industry and its proximity to the townships, in a district of previously unspoiled countryside. The press reports were short and insignificant.

> "On Tuesday, No. 1 furnace at Coatham Ironworks was tapped for the first time, having been put in blast the previous morning. No. 2 furnace will be blown today."
>
> *Redcar and Saltburn News,* 12th June, 1873.

It is difficult to ascertain the number employed at the ironworks in those early days; a newspaper report of 1895 states that there were around two hundred men at the Redcar Ironworks. The census of 1881 will show the breakdown of the trades and the origins of newcomers to the district. However, as this information remains secret for 100 years, the exact results of the census will not be made public until 1982. Some of the new iron-workers no doubt came from the building trades. By 1876, building was in recession at the two resorts as the initial explosion of development had petered out; many bricklayers, joiners and labourers could utilise their skills equally well in the ironworks. A number of Irish Roman Catholics had moved to the district seeking work, coincidental with the beginnings of the iron industry, the first Catholic school and church were built in Redcar. From living memory, there are recollections of skilled men coming from Staffordshire.

Blast furnacemen worked an average of eighty-four hours each week until almost the end of the nineteenth century. They worked a twelve-hour shift six days a week, with a twenty-four hour shift alternate Saturdays. The twenty-four hour shift, or "long turn", made possible the change over of shifts. Once each fortnight the men had Sunday off. There were no other holidays. In the early days, the work was not continuous and the pace was slow, otherwise the men could never have coped with the long hours or withstood the working conditions. Technical innovations in the 1880's speeded up the process considerably. Men throughout Cleveland demanded a three shift system. A decade later, 1897, most of the companies in Cleveland adopted the standard eight-hour shift.

The Cleveland iron industry was at its peak when Redcar and Coatham Ironworks were built. A depression followed, bringing hardship to the ironworkers and their families.

> "Attention was called to the great amount of distress at present prevailing in the town (Redcar). The surveyor was empowered to obtain a supply of unbroken blue flint for road-making purposes and to employ any men who applied, to break the stone."
> *The Middlesbrough News and Cleveland Advertiser,*
> 9th March, 1878.

A year later, the same paper carried the following:

> "Attention has been drawn to the continued, serious distress among the poor of Redcar. Upwards of £50 has already been

dispensed by the church wardens in food, coals, and money: and the Wesleyans have distributed soup and bread twice a week."

Later in the century, in 1892, the strike by the Durham miners brought more suffering to the whole of Cleveland. The strike lasted three months and during that time every ironworker and miner was thrown out of work through no fault of his own. By the third week of the strike, the *Evening Gazette* reported that all the furnaces at Redcar had been damped down and the men were laid off. They were luckier than many, as the owners, Walker, Maynard and Company allowed the tenants of the firm's fifty houses at Warrenby, to live rent free for the duration of the strike. Downeys, owners of the Coatham furnaces had been in financial trouble since the depression and their two furnaces had been out of blast for some years. Around the turn of the century, they sold out to Walker, Maynard and Company. In 1915, Walker Maynard's ironworks were taken over by Dorman Long and from then on they were known as the Warrenby Works.

WARRENBY

BY September, 1873, a new village was emerging on the Kirkleatham Estate to house the ironworkers and their families. "Where is Warrentown?" asks the *Redcar and Saltburn News* on 25th September, 1873. Then it continues, giving a favourable report of the newly formed village. The cottages were erected by Messrs. Robson, Maynard and Company on the main thoroughfare called Tod Point Road. They were impressive and reported as being of a standard above the common run of workmen's dwellings. Built in terraces of seven, each cottage had a small garden under the front window and a neat iron railing between the garden and the pavement. Downey and Coney Streets were also mentioned in the newspaper report. The land was leased from Mr. A. H. Turner of Kirkleatham Hall. Warrenby virtually exploded into existence with almost the entire village being built in a single wave of development. Building sites were everywhere. Some two hundred sites had been leased, a site reserved for a school and a large hotel was being built. To the south of Tod Point Road, the land was laid out in small gardens so that each occupier might grow his own potatoes and keep a pig. The village later changed its name to Warrenby as it was thought that the 'by' suffix was more in keeping with the many Danish influenced place names in Cleveland.

SACRED HEART CHURCH

BEFORE the 1870's, there were perhaps only around thirty members of the Roman Catholic Church living in Redcar. With the opening of the ironworks came many Irishmen and their families seeking work, bringing with them strong Catholic beliefs. In 1874, Canon Riddell held services at a small church in Lord Street. Three years later a new place of worship was opened for the Roman Catholic community. The first church of the Sacred Heart was built in Thrush Road and accommodated two hundred and twenty worshippers. Forty years later, the new Sacred Heart Church was opened in Lobster Road and the old building was passed on to the Methodist Church who still use it today.

CHAPTER SEVEN — 1876 - 1880
KIRKLEATHAM LOCAL BOARD OF HEALTH

AFTER the founding of the ironworks, the population of Coatham more than doubled, increasing from 1,615 in 1872 to 3,300 in 1876. Yet for all its rising importance, Coatham was still governed by Guisborough Rural Sanitary Authority. There was a growing feeling of dissatisfaction among the ratepayers of Coatham at this state of affairs. Having become a community of some stature and importance they felt that the governing powers should be placed in their own hands. A meeting of ratepayers was held in Coatham in 1876, to consider whether it was advisable to form a local board for the district of Kirkleatham. There was one notable absentee from the large, well-supported meeting; Mr. Newcomen of Kirkleatham was strongly in favour of the proposed local board, but did not wish to appear in the proceedings so that the ratepayers could feel free to arrive at a decision of their own accord. Financially, there was the question of whether or not they were willing to pay a rate of two pence in the pound and have the government in their own care. If they were not prepared to pay, then Guisborough Rural Sanitary Authority would remain in control.

As Redcar and Coatham had similar interests and common problems, it was proposed that a joint board be formed with Redcar. Due to the proximity of the two towns, indeed they merged together now, one surveyor, one clerk and one board room would suffice for both. The idea was rejected outright. Coatham was larger in population than its neighbour and it was common knowledge that the Redcar Local Board was in debt. A feeling of "them" and "us" was born and was to dominate many issues for the next half century. A poll was demanded. The results showed a large majority in favour of the formation of a local board for Coatham. A Local Government Inquiry was held in the National School in Coatham in July, 1876. The inspector was presented with the following resolutions which had been approved by a meeting of ratepayers:

"It is undesirable to separate or divide the parish in any way . . ."

"It is impolitic to attempt a union with the district of Redcar, especially as they have entirely different services of water supply and drainage. Also there is strong local feeling in the parish against such a union."

Then the evidence in favour of the proposed board was presented to the inspector. There were figures showing the increase in the population and the growth in the number of houses in the preceding four years. Mr. Newcomen added his support publicly. Recognising the difficulty of working efficiently from a distance, Guisborough Rural Sanitary Authority approved the proposition. There was a unanimous feeling among the ratepayers in favour of the new board. They sought greater powers to control the standards of building and the laying out of the streets and of the general sanitary arrangements of the town. They were also unanimous in wanting nothing to do with Redcar; Coatham was the select community, Redcar was a grubby, ill-planned resort.

"That difference was what the stranger failed to see," said the inspector. On entering Redcar he had seen a fence and been told that it was the boundary between the two towns. Without it he could see just one town, with but a common interest. The meeting could not agree with the inspector's observation. Coatham was residential, Redcar was a place of business; there were different classes of people either side of the fence. A novel reason for the separate boards, thought the inspector. He then clarified a misunderstanding; if united under a common board, Kirkleatham would not be involved in solving the debt of Redcar's existing board.

In November of the same year, Redcar Local Board of Health received the report of the Local Government Board Inspector. The report favoured the amalgamation of Redcar and Kirkleatham, The new board would have fifteen members, six from Redcar and nine from Coatham. Thus the new district of Coatham would take control of its established neighbour. Fearing amongst other points, a loss of control, a rise in rates and being unable to find any advantages in the proposal, the Redcar Board unanimously opposed it. No immediate decision was made. The local Government Board wanted to look further into the feelings of the people of Redcar and Coatham. The two towns agreed to differ. At a meeting of the ratepayers from both sides of the fence, a unanimous decision was reached—against amalgamation.

In July, 1877, the provisional order was received constituting the Parish of Kirkleatham into a Local Board district and an election was arranged for 1st September. There were thirty candidates from whom the following nine were elected:

Thomas D. Ridley, contractor; John Proud, farmer; James Rutherford, land agent; Edward Robson, mine owner; John Hikeley, inn-keeper; Thomas James, ironworks manager; Arthur H. T. Newcomen, Gentleman; Peter Wallis, farmer; Wm. Nelson, builder. Arthur Henry Turner Newcomen was unanimously elected Chairman.

The Kirkleatham Local Board of Health wasted little time in taking hold of the reins. It first met in the Lobster Inn in November, 1877. Subsequently meetings were held in the National school. The chairman of the Board was very much the father of Coatham as we know it. Due to his foresight, the sanitary arrangements were good, having been laid down to his plans in 1865. He had also exercised strict control, prior to the Board's creation, over buildings. Such was his influence that the streets between Queen Street and the sea were to be named Arthur, Henry, Turner and Newcomen streets. Water was supplied to most of the Kirkleatham Parish from the Stockton and Middlesbrough Water Company. The Inspector from the Local Government Board remarked that Coatham was more modern, better laid out and had better width of streets, more regular buildings and better footways, than its poor relation.

An early task for the Board was to arrange for the scavenging of the night soil from the privies. Tenders were invited for the work and the manure was to belong to the Board and to be sold by auction. The year was 1877. The following year the Board undertook to clean the streets and arrange with the Water Company for a supply of water for this purpose. In February, 1878, the sewers were improved by the addition of six ventilators. One still stands, a high cast-iron pipe, at the junction of Queen Street and Newcomen Terrace.

Relationships between the two neighbouring Boards appeared to improve little over the years. In 1879 they agreed to purchase a fire engine to serve both towns but the joint venture was, predictably, doomed to failure. Four years later, the Minute Book of the Kirkleatham Board records :

> "As the Redcar Local Board have refused to confirm the rules and Regulations of the joint Fire Brigade, the Fire Engine Committee is to be dissolved and immediate steps are to be taken to purchase and house a fire engine and organise a fire brigade at the expense of this district alone."

The fire station, originally in Kirkleatham Street, moved to a new building in Pierson Street in 1912. This became a Cleansing Depot when the Brigade moved to Coatham Road in 1943. The latest move, to the Trunk Road, was in 1963.

REDCAR LOCAL BOARD OF HEALTH

IN the summer of 1870, smallpox broke out in Redcar and quickly spread throughout the town. A local doctor opined that the epidemic might have been prevented by prompt action from the Local Board of Health. Initially the Board took no action. When the first case came to the doctor's attention, he reported it to the Board asking for money to employ a nurse. He received no response. "Had it been otherwise I would have no hesitation in stating that it would have prevented what afterwards developed into a severe epidemic simply from the fact that the case had to be nursed by his relatives and willing friends who, not understanding my caution, surreptitiously gave their aid," wrote the frustrated doctor in the Evening Gazette. Finding themselves in the middle of an epidemic, the Local Board called a meeting of medical men, to ask advice; by then, though, the disease was prevalent in all parts of the town. Some good did come from the sorry episode. Realising the importance of prevention of disease, the Board appointed a Medical Officer of Health for Redcar. He was to advise on precautions that might be taken to forestall further outbreaks of disease.

The minute books record the reports of the annual inspections into the town's sanitary conditions. The report of 1872 states:

"After careful house to house visitation in which every ash pit, privy, sink and W.C. was examined, we have to report that the sanitary condition of Redcar is better than we have been accustomed to find it at similar annual inspections. The few exceptional cases are those of old property built before the existence of the Local Board. The yards are too small and so the privy and ash pit accommodation are inadequate."

The landlords were ordered to make the necessary improvements. The report went on to emphasise the need for a public scavenger and concluded:

"If these improvements are carried out, the sanitary condition of Redcar will be found in all respects satisfactory."

The inspector was in a delicate position; to criticise the conditions too severely was to imply neglect of purpose by the Board which employed him. The state of Redcar was still far from satisfactory and a further two decades were to pass before conditions generally became acceptable.

In 1876, Redcar applied for an extension of the district to include that part of the town which still came under the care of Upleatham; this was granted a year later in accordance with the petition of the Local Board of Health.

REDCAR RACECOURSE

HORSE races had been held on the sands at Redcar for many years. Local sportsmen competed for small prizes — a saddle, a bridle or a few sovereigns. A bathing machine served for the judge's box and a farm wagon for the stewards. Feeling that horse racing at Redcar had greater potential, an enterprising group formed the Race Committee in the middle of the 1800's. Its purpose was to introduce racing on more ambitions lines. Sufficient money was raised to offer stakes large enough to attract competitors from further afield, from Middleham, Richmond, Malton and Hambleton. The venture was a success. Redcar Races gained a new status and were included in the Racing Calendar. The races continued to be held on the sands until 1870 when they could no longer be held there for financial reasons.

The Race Committee leased land from the Newcomen family. The present racecourse was laid out in 1871 and the first meeting was held in 1872. Admission charges were two pence to the course and six shillings to the Grandstand enclosure. Three years later, the Redcar and Coatham Grandstand Company was formed. Their first decision was to build a new stand worthy of the meeting, this would replace the wooden stand which was dismantled after each meeting. During the same year, the course was improved. Arrangements were made with the Earl of Zetland for the extension of the course allowing for the inclusion of a straight mile in the course; this gave some added prestige to Racing at Redcar. Until the turn of the century, most prize money was about £100; total prize money in 1946 was £8,450 and in 1964 it had risen to £72,550, and in 1976 it topped £133,500.

The firm foundations and the early, and continuing success, of Redcar Races is attributed by the late Major J. Fairfax Blakeborough to the loyalty and enthusiasm of the local landowners— the Zetlands, the Newcomens and the Lowthers of Wilton. Since the Second World War, Redcar has led the world with innovations which have become accepted as the standards now; the publicly visible timing clock, the furlong posts, closed circuit television in colour are but a few.

THE PIERS

THE Redcar Pier Company was formed in 1866 with the intention of "providing Redcar with a commodious promenade and landing pier. The plans lay dormant until 1870 when a rival scheme for Coatham was proposed. A suggestion that a central pier be built to benefit both towns was never actively pursued. Each group wanted the pier sited in their town; a compromise proved impossible, each resolved to build its own pier.

Redcar's scheme was financed by the selling of shares and, of course, the Earl of Zetland made a generous donation. The first pile was driven by Admiral Chaloner of Guisborough on 28th August, 1871, and the structure erected by Messrs. Head Wrightson of Stockton. The completed pier was 1,300 feet long and stemmed from the Esplanade, opposite Clarendon Street. The entrance was twenty feet wide and the gates were flanked by toll-collectors' offices and ladies' and gentlemen's rooms and a shop. The pier head was 114 feet wide and featured a bandstand with sheltered seating for seven hundred. There was a small landing stage at the pier head from which paddle steamers ran pleasure cruises

Redcar Pier Head 1880

along the coast and plied regularly between Middlesbrough, Redcar, Saltburn and Whitby, Bridlington and Scarborough.

Shareholders had their hopes of regular dividends dashed by a succession of mishaps. At the end of October, 1880, the brig *Luna*, driven by storms, cut through the pier. Repairs cost the pier company £1,000. On New Year's Eve, 1885, the S.S. *Cochrane* demolished the landing stage and the pier company was unable to bear the cost of the repairs. Further damage occurred in January, 1897, when wreckage from the schooner *Amarant* swept against the pier stanchions. The most damaging blow came in the summer of 1898. Late on the night of August 20th fire broke out and the pier head was burnt down following a concert party. It was believed that the fire was caused by a wax vesta which had fallen, unextinguished between the planks. The bandstand was not rebuilt but was replaced by a mobile bandstand on the promenade. The total damage bill was between £1,000 and £1,500. In 1907 a pavillion housing a large ballroom was built near the entrance to the pier. It was extended landwards in 1928 and the minaret kiosks were absorbed into the frontage of the ballroom.

A deliberate breach was made in the pier in 1940. This was to hinder the enemy in the event of invasion. During the War, a mine exploded near the pier considerably weakening the structure which was already much decayed through neglect. After that, succeeding storms washed away almost the entire structure. The stump of the once magnificent pier projected only some fifteen yards beyond the Pier Ballroom, and remains much as we see it today.

Coatham pier was intended to outstrip Redcar by some 700 feet. Originally planned to be 2,000 feet long, it had the dubious distinction of being wrecked before it was completed. Work commenced in 1873. In December, 1874, two vessels collided with it. The brig *Griffin* was running north before a storm with a cargo of oak; the lashing wind and rain reduced visibility and the crew failed to see the unfinished seaward end of the pier. As the vessel slewed through, the crew escaped by jumping on to the pier. Later in the same storm, the schooner *Corrymbus* was driven through the pier and was a total loss. The cost of repairing the work was such that it was deemed wiser to shorten the pier by 200 feet to reduce the overall cost. The work was completed and the pier opened in 1875. It had two pavilions, one in the middle for band concerts and one near the entrance which housed a roller skating rink.

The pier joined the sea front opposite Station Road, then Newcomen Street. It continued to be dogged by misfortune and its demise came in October, 1898, when it was almost completely wrecked by the barque *Birger*. The Coatham Pier Company, already in financial difficulties through the cost of earlier repairs, could not afford further repairs on the large scale necessary to restore the pier. Instead they dismantled the severed, seaward portion. The following year the Pier Company ceased trading and the pier was allowed to disintegrate.

At the beginning of the present century, the then local authority erected a glass shelter over the old skating rink and gave the place a new lease of life as "Cosy Corner", the home for some years of Billy Scarrow's pierrots. In 1928 the "glasshouse" as it was known (a description still heard occasionally in 1980) was rebuilt as a theatre and called the New Pavilion. When the old Central Hall with its cinemas was demolished on 23rd July, 1964, the "New Pav" was converted into the Regent Cinema.

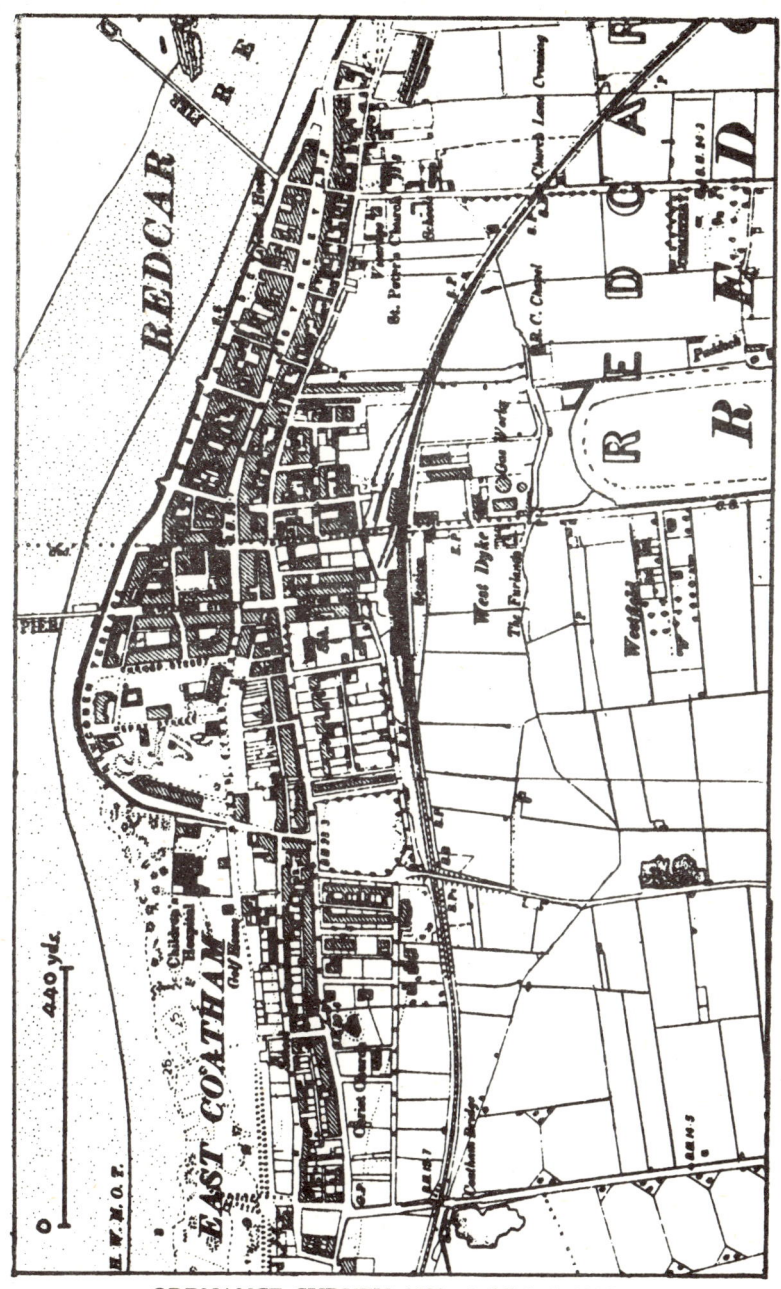

ORDNANCE SURVEY 1893, Published 1895
Part of 1: 10,560 Sheet Yorks., N. Riding VII N.E.
Reduced in size from original scale.

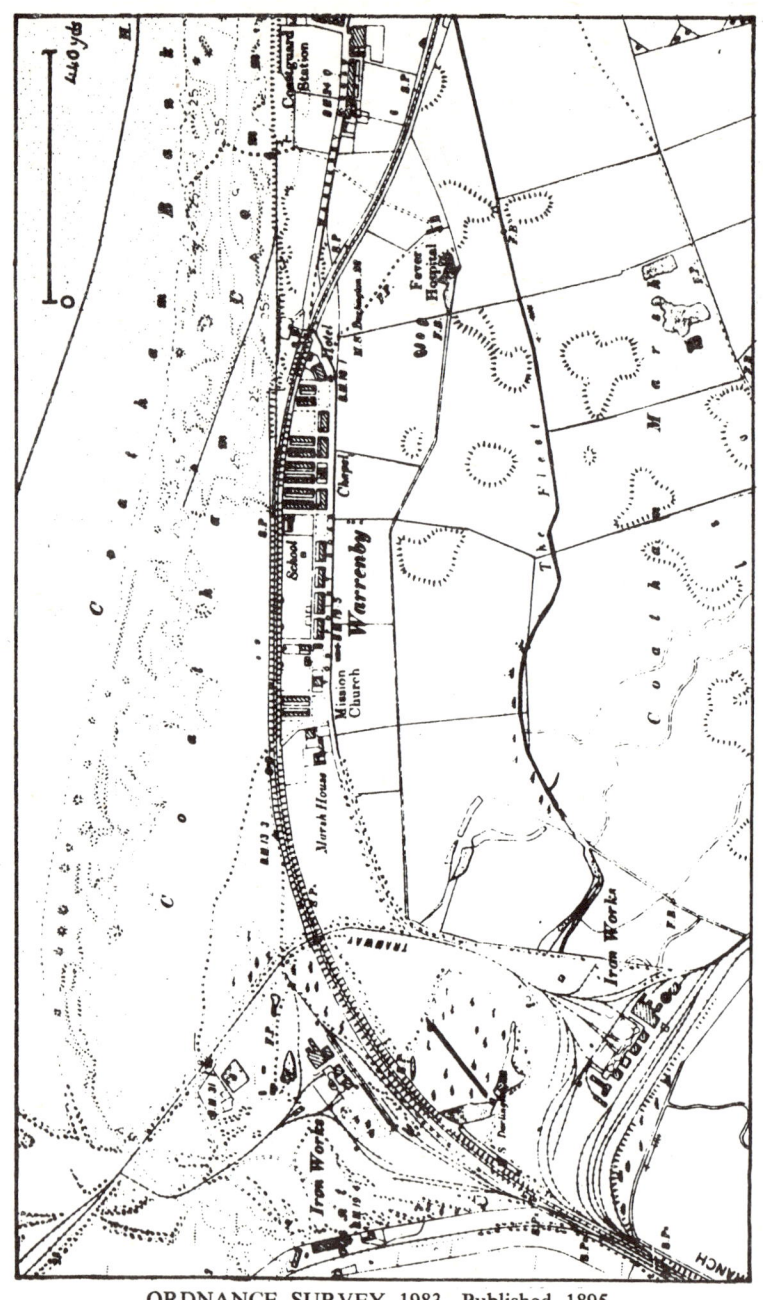

ORDNANCE SURVEY 1983, Published 1895
Part of 1 : 10,560 Sheet Yorks., N. Riding VII N.W.
Reduced in size from original scale.

CHAPTER EIGHT — 1881 - 1900

THE second Ordnance Survey Map of the district was published in 1895 and it presents the last officially published picture of the area in the 19th century. By then, Coatham had been more or less built up as far as the railway line. Several terraces had been built south of Coatham Road. Overlooking the cricket ground was Trafalgar Terrace and behind that, St. Vincent's Terrace. Along Kirkleatham Street were several villas which now form the Stead Memorial Hospital. Another new street was Westbourne Grove and construction was under way in Henry Street and Turner Street. Few new working class dwellings were built in Coatham, there were only two short terraces of ironworkers cottages—Grant Street and North Terrace, which were demolished in 1978.

The building of working class homes was more widespread in Redcar. Almost all the new cottages were built in the four years 1872-76; this was the time during which the ironworks was being established. During this time, existing rows were completed in Alma Parade, Albert and Wilton Streets and Cleveland Terrace (the latter is now Railway Terrace). A number of new streets were planned in 1873-74. North of the railway line work started on Red Lion and Regent Streets and Regent and Fairbridge Places. South of the railway there were Birdsall Row and Herschell and Elton Streets. There was also new building work in Portland Terrace in West Dyke Road.

The building boom was over by the spring of 1876. Then followed a recession in the building trades until 1893. During those years Redcar changed very little. The new streets were laid out but not completely developed; Elton Street had only four houses and Birdsall Row had none according to the Ordnance map. The decline in the iron trade in the 1880's and the miners' strike of 1892 had brought the town's growth to an abrupt halt. What development there was, was closely controlled by the Local Board which insisted on its conditions being met and the bye-laws observed. The plans for Red Lion Street had been rejected five times, amongst the reasons given, it was pointed out that the proposed roadway was only twenty-four feet wide and the bye-laws required thirty feet. The sixth plan was approved in May, 1873, the year following the original application for planning approval.

JOHN SPEAR'S REPORT

IN 1885 a *Special Report on the Sanitary Condition of Redcar —with reference to its state of preparedness to withstand the invasion of cholera* was prepared by John Spears. The report deals initially with the defects in the sanitary arrangements. There was criticism of the haphazard way in which the sewers had been laid out and of their poor ventilation. Due to the flatness of the land, there was very little fall on the sewers. To keep the channels free, catch pits had been inserted and were emptied only once or twice each month. These pits were malodorous and ill-maintained. Some branch sewers were rendered even less efficient by acumulations of deposits. Private drainage needed considerable alteration. It was recommended that drain pipes be removed from within or beneath dwellings. Water closets were still found only in the better properties and the larger lodging houses. In the poorer parts of the town privy middens were still in general use, often in a "very dilapidated and foul condition." There were a few pail closets which were a slight improvement on the middens. Some arrangements had been made for refuse disposal but scavenging of the privies was not dealt with systematically; often calls were only made after complaints.

The water supply was, on the whole good, although sometimes insufficient. Much water was lost through the leaky and worn out mains. There were still a few local wells but these supplies were of doubtful quality.

The poorer dwellings were in a most unsatisfactory state. Many were very damp, some were so delapidated as to be classed as unfit for human habitation. There were several very small cottages which were overcrowded. Many of the newer houses and cottages for the artisans were found to be jerry-built. In the poorer parts of the town, the yards were described as filthy and dilapidated. There were several undedicated streets which had not been adopted by the Local Board. Common lodging houses were not registered in any way and were regulated by the police. They were all found to be overcrowded, ill-ventilated and dirty.

Criticism was levelled at the Local Board of Redcar itself. Its work was inefficent, its bye-laws were outdated and inadequate. The Medical Officer of Health was old, feeble and underpaid. His reports were meagre and of no value. The work performed by the Inspector of Nuisances was "as fair as can be expected under the circumstances." There was neither a hospital nor ambulance in the town and no arrangements had been made in anticipation of cholera striking.

Later in the same year, John Spears turned his attention towards the conditions in Kirkleatham District. The report implies that generally Coatham was in a better state than Redcar. The homes of the poor were as a rule "fair"; there were many complaints of dampness in the older property. There were no cases of overcrowding in the poorer households and there were no common lodging houses in Coatham. The sewers were kept free of accumulated deposits by regular flushing but their ventilation needed improving. Spears criticised the layout of some parts of the town; some small blocks of dwellings were so arranged as to restrict the free circulation of air. In one or two instances yards had been built over.

Turning to the activities of the Sanitary Authority and its officers, Spears' report is word for word the same as his report on Redcar. As in Redcar, he found neither hospital, ambulance nor any plans for dealing with cholera.

Acting on Spears' report, in December, 1885, Redcar Local Board of Health entered in its minutes that it intended taking steps to borrow money to finance various public works. The money would be spent on, amongst other things, replacing the water main from the reservoir to the town and a scheme for supplying the town with salt water for cleaning the streets and flushing the sewers. In March, 1886, the Clerk was instructed to serve notice upon the owners of property in the following streets to level, pave, flag and channel them: Alma Parade, Red Lion, Regent, Wilton and Back Streets and Wilton Place. Most important of all, the Board began to take more vigorous action against the owners of insanitary property on the following lines:

> "Notice to be served on —— ——, owner of cottages 40 and 51 Lord Street, because the property is damp and dilapidated."

> "Notice to be served on —— ——, stating that his eight houses in Smith Street are in such a state as to be unfit for human habitation."

In the latter case, the owner was given twenty-one days to make improvements, in default of which, proceedings would be taken to prohibit the use of the premises for human habitation. The main improvement in Coatham's sanitary condition was in the arrangements concerning the privies. The Kirkleatham Local Board of Health recommended that the pan system should be adopted in all cases where nuisances were reported from privies or ashpits. As a result of this, notices were served on owners of property in Station Road, Pierson Street and Pierson's Buildings requiring them to provide ash pans. The Kirkleatham Board also took steps to provide a hospital. In 1888 a house known as the Weigh House was converted to be used as a Fever Hospital; the building stood in isolation, well back from the road between Coatham and Warrenby.

In September, 1892, came a special report from the Local Government Board concerning the threat of cholera. Attention was drawn to the fact that Redcar still had no accommodation for isolating cases of infectious disease. The Board was prepared to wait until it was absolutely necessary before spending money. Six years passed before isolation accommodation was provided for Redcar, then only when the Board was spurred into action by the threat of an epidemic. In 1898 smallpox was raging through Middlesbrough and the neighbouring towns. To no-one's surprise, the Medical Officer of Health of Redcar eventually received notification of a case of smallpox in his district.

The advisability of isolating the case was discussed and it was decided to act jointly with Saltburn and Marske Councils and provide a joint hospital for the people of all three towns. A site was suggested on Hob Hill at Saltburn, well isolated and with plenty of fresh air. Saltburn Board were not fired with enthusiasm at the proposition. As they saw it, there was already a case at Redcar, though none at Saltburn. If the case was isolated at Saltburn, it would be said, rightly enough, that there was smallpox in the town, which might damage its image. Moreover, if there were many cases from Redcar, the hospital may have to be enlarged and Saltburn would have to bear some of the cost, even though none of the cases came from their own district. Finally the Marske deputation suggested a site at the foot of the Upleatham Hills (near the junction of the A174 and Redcar Lane). This location was well isolated and readily accessible from Marske, Redcar and Saltburn. The site was approved and plans were passed immediately for a building of wood and corrugated iron to accommodate six patients. The building was erected within the week. The case was isolated and the epidemic averted.

ENTERIC FEVER IN COATHAM

IN 1893 Doctor Barry reported to the Local Government Board on *Enteric Fever in the Tees Valley Towns*. There had been two outbreaks, each lasting about six weeks; 7th September to 18th October, 1890, and, after a brief respite, from 28th December to 7th February, 1891. There had been hundreds of cases of enteric fever in Middlesbrough and Stockton, causing the death rates of those towns to rise alarmingly. Other districts affected included Darlington, Ormesby, Normanby and Eston, the rural districts of Stockton, and Kirkleatham district which included Coatham of course. Dr. Barry made a careful and detailed examination into the sanitary conditions of each of the affected districts.

In Kirkleatham, he noted first the character of the district. The inhabitants of Warrenby and Dunsdale were employed chiefly in the ironworks and ironstone mines; those of Kirkleatham village worked on the land; Coatham he described as a residential resort with much rented accommodation. These activities were reflected in the type and mixture of housing in each community. At Dunsdale and Warrenby most of the dwellings were classed as cottages; at Coatham, less than a quarter of the houses were for the working class. Dr. Barry found the town of Coatham to be well laid out, with most of the houses of a superior class. As a rule there was sufficient space around each house; however, he too noticed that in some parts of the town there were blocks of houses placed so closely as to restrict the movement of fresh air and that yards had been built over. He found the main roads in the district had been macadamised and apparently well kept. The back streets of Coatham were satisfactory but at Warrenby "they were unpaved, unmade, unswept and frequently filthy." Little fault was found with the sewers and Barry reports that they were flushed with salt water daily in summer and twice weekly in winter. Most of the houses in Coatham had flush toilets, the rest of the district had midden privies or pans.

Water for all the houses in Coatham and Warrenby came from the Tees through the works of the Stockton and Middlesbrough Water Board. The villages of Dunsdale, Kirkleatham and Yearby, and all the outlying farms were dependent on wells and streams for their supply. This was the crucial factor. All the incidents of disease in Kirkleatham district occurred in Coatham and Warrenby; not a single case was reported at the villages of Kirkleatham, Yearby and Dunsdale. In every district where the disease struck there was a single, obvious common factor, the Tees. It was noted that the outbreaks both followed heavy flooding of the river. The Tees acted as a common sewer for all the places along its banks. Dr. Barry commented :

> " At Barnard Castle almost everything had been contrived so as to ensure, to the fullest, the fouling of the river by every conceivable form of filth."

The scene was also visited by the Kirkleatham Board of Health and they reported in detail in their minute book of June, 1893 :

> " We found on the Durham side large accumulations of filth of every description, such as ash pits refuse and human excrement from privies and closets, also several drains discharging into the river."

The Yorkshire side was just as deplorable. They also found "a huge heap of rubbish looking for all the world like a giant ash pit." Their final comment :

> " From looking at the high water mark on the bank, it is certain that all the filth will be washed into the stream at the first flood and carried to the Stockton and Middlesbrough pumping station."

COATHAM'S WATER SUPPLY

FOR some years, the Kirkleatham Local Board had received complaints about the inadequate water supply in the district. Drains were not always effectively flushed and there were many complaints of bad smells. The water pressure was insufficient for water to reach water closets on the upper floors of the lodging houses, particularly worrying in warm weather when the houses were full of visitors. Coatham was at its peak as a resort and its reputation as a healthy place was important.

Correspondence with the Stockton and Middlesbrough Water Board proved ineffectual. The Kirkleatham Board decided to transfer its supply from Stockton and Middlesbrough to the Cleveland Water Board. They applied for the sanction of the Local Government Board to borrow money with which to purchase the pipes, mains and fittings within the district belonging to the Stockton and Middlesbrough Company. When the first application was refused, further attempts were made, much emphasis being laid on Dr. Barry's report and the effect of Tees water in causing the fever outbreaks. Eventually consent was obtained.

The Kirkleatham Local Board served a notice on the Stockton and Middlesbrough Water Board compelling them to sell all the mains, pipes and fittings within the district. There followed a legal struggle. The Water Board rejected the offer made by the Kirkleatham Board of £2,669. An arbitrator was appointed by the Local Government Board; after hearing both parties he fixed the price at £25,422. The arbitrator had based his award on the revenue which the Water Board would have received from Kirkleatham, not on the actual value of the equipment. Shocked, the Kirkleatham Board appealed to the High Court and their appeal was upheld. The Water Board then appealed against the findings of the High Court; on 31st July, 1893, their appeal was dismissed by the House of Lords. Arrangements were swiftly made and from August, 1893, the Kirkleatham District received its water from the reservoir at Lockwood Beck, through the works of the Cleveland Water Company.

THE WARRENBY BOILER EXPLOSION

A TERRIFIC explosion shook the district on the 14th June, 1895. At Redcar Ironworks, thirteen boilers had exploded killing four men outright and injuring many more, some fatally.

The explosion came at about supper time. The furnaces had been tapped and many of the men were in their cabins for the first meal of the night shift. One of the boilers overheated, causing a seam to rip, and then exploded. A chain reaction followed as boilers, weakened by the first blast, exploded hurling metal, bricks and masonry high in the air. Men were buried under the rubble. Others were caught in jets of steam or scalded with showers of boiling water.

In Warrenby they first heard a low rumbling, followed by a low thud. Eye witnesses saw a huge globular cloud rising from the works. There was much alarm and the whole village rushed to the works. Bodies were to be seen everywhere. Rescuers were surprised to find so few dead; but many of the injured were badly maimed. Doctors and nurses worked all night alongside the rescuers administering what aid they could to those who had been scalded and crushed. The injured were taken to the Cottage Hospital at North Ormesby.

The death toll mounted to eleven as the days passed, the local men were buried in Coatham churchyard. At the inquest it was said that the explosion was unparalleled in the country. The verdict was "death from injuries resulting from the bursting of a boiler which had become overheated." No negligence was found on the part of the company regarding the maintenance of the boilers.

THE WRECK OF THE "AMARANT"

REDCAR has its own *Marie Celeste* story. In the early hours of the morning of Tuesday, 12th January, 1897, the Norwegian brig Amarant loaded with oak, was seen drifting between the two piers of Redcar and Coatham. Warnings went unheeded. Several Redcar fishermen boarded her; they found the lights burning but no-one else aboard.

The Amarant had been abandoned during dense fog and had drifted at the mercy of the wind and tide until eventually coming ashore at Redcar. The crew of the abandoned vessel had been picked up by a passing steamer bound for the Tees. Having been deserted, the wreck became the property of the fishermen who brought her to the beach. No doubt the oak was put to many uses locally. A week later the Amarant was broken up in a storm and only her hull remained. The following day, the hull was driven by the storm through Redcar pier, making a breach in the pier eighty yards wide.

THE WRECK OF THE "BIRGER"

THE barque Birger met a tragic fate on Saltscar rocks. Loaded with salt she had sprung a leak near the Dogger Bank, a hundred miles away. Flamborough Head was the nearest land, yet it took four days through gales to sight it. The furious seas prevented the barque making land. Word was sent along the storm lashed coast of the vessel's distress. Scarborough and Runswick Bay lifeboats were unable to assist. Whitby lifeboat was standing by but the waterlogged craft was driven three miles offshore as she passed the port. Word reached Redcar ahead of the Birger on 22nd October, 1898.

Several thousand people were gathered to witness the sad spectacle. Crashing over Saltscar, her masts snapped and both the captain and the chief officer were killed by the falling debris. The national lifeboat, The Brothers, was hauled down to the beach and rowed out through the mountainous seas. Dismasted, all that remained of the luckless vessel was the hull with the helpless crew clinging to it for their lives. Cheers went up from Coatham Pier as a piece of wreckage with three men clinging to it, was swept towards the pier. Ropes were lowered and as the makeshift raft passed under the pier one man was hauled to safety. A second clambered up then, nearing the top, fell back exhausted, to his death in the foaming sea. The third was washed away, then thrown by the sea on to the beach and revived. Only these two of the crew of fifteen lived. Had the vessel been able to run ashore, the Rocket Brigade could have saved the crew by firing lifelines from the shore, across the vessel. The wreck broke through Coatham pier, leaving a gap a hundred yards wide and came to rest on Coatham sands.

The following day, wreckage was strewn for miles along the beaches and as was their custom, many of the locals were there picking up anything that might be of value or use. The coastguards were unable to patrol the scattered wreckage and prevent the pilferage. A sad ending to a brave attempt to reach safety. Months later, a letter was received from Finland thanking the people of Redcar who had sent Christmas gifts to the bereaved families of the crew of the Birger.

THE AMALGAMATION

THE initiative for amalgamating the two boards came from Kirkleatham. The Redcar Local Board resolutely opposed the idea to the bitter end. In 1887, the Kirkleatham Board first brought the matter before the Local Government Board, claiming that they were acting in response to a petition which they had received.

The petition in favour of amalgamating the Boards was signed by a large number of the ratepayers of both districts. Redcar challenged the validity of the petition. They claimed that many of the signatures had been obtained under false pretences and that many who had signed the petition were now anxious to sign a petition opposing the move. The Redcar Board then passed a resolution opposing the motion, embodying the following points :

> The majority of the property owners and large ratepayers were against the amalgamation.
> Only two members of Redcar's Board were in favour.

The Earl of Zetland was against it.

The Board could see no advantage in such a change.

In 1894 there was a change in the formation of local government; Urban District Councils replaced the Local Boards of Health. That same year, Kirkleatham U.D.C. made a further application to the North Riding County Council. The new Redcar U.D.C. still considered the proposed change "neither desirable nor necessary." A committee was appointed to oppose any move to bring about amalgamation.

When the County Council reached its decision, it was certainly not to the liking of Kirkleatham U.D.C. In 1896, by order of the County Council, the parish of Kirkleatham was to be divided into two separate parishes. Coatham was to be amalgamated with Redcar; Kirkleatham, Yearby and Dunsdale were to revert to the control of Guisborough Rural Sanitary Authority. There was an outcry from all concerned. The right of appeal to the Local Government Board was promptly exercised. An inquiry was held at the Coatham Hotel on 21st April, 1897, and as a result, the original order was not confirmed. The following year, an amended order was made by the County Council. This too was resisted but it was becoming accepted that the amalgamation was inevitable. On Wednesday, 1st March, 1899, the communities of Redcar and Coatham were united under one Urban District Council. There were twelve councillors, six from each ward. The union of the rivals was further cemented when the continued growth of the town, early in the twentieth century, merited the transition to the status of Municipal Borough Council.

No public celebrations marked the turn of the century, yet the nineteenth century had probably been the most important in the history of Redcar and Coatham. Both had remained unchanged for a millenium, two quiet fishing villages, their existence barely noticed by the outside world. The nineteenth century had brought social and industrial changes undreamt of. Both communities had come of age and been well and truly wedded.

CHAPTER NINE — 1900 - 1914
THE TOWN MATURES

REDCAR and Coatham entered the twentieth century as a united township with a combined population of almost 8,000. The population continued to grow at a substantial but steady rate.

TOTAL POPULATION FIGURES — REDCAR & COATHAM
1901	—	7,675
1911	—	10,503
1921	—	16,401
1931	—	20,159

A census was not conducted in 1941

Having prospered in the nineteenth century as a popular resort, Redcar matured in the twentieth century as a desirable residential town.

With Britain still in the throes of the Boer War, the turn of the century had passed quietly. In November 1900 it was decided to erect a memorial to the Redcar volunteers who had been killed in the South African Campaign. A specially inscribed tombstone was laid in Redcar Cemetery over the grave of Wilson Wiles. The inscription states that Corporal Wiles, of the Yorkshire Regiment was wounded at Paadeberg in South Africa and taken as a prisoner of war. He died at Netley Hospital, aged 22 years. The stone also bears the names of Privates Hardy and Wilkinson, who were killed at Paadeberg, and Private Outhwaite who died of enteric fever. The Boer War ended in 1902 and news of peace reached Redcar in the morning newspapers on 2nd June. The local schools were given a holiday. The children of Redcar, together with their teachers and the Vicar, assembled in the High Street and sang the National Anthem. The High Street was a blaze of colour with flags and bunting hung out in jubilation.

THE DEATH OF QUEEN VICTORIA

The old Queen passed away in January 1901. The sad news reached Redcar during the evening of 22nd January. It was announced to the town by the tolling of church bells. The following morning, flags were set at half-mast at the Council Office, the Constitutional Club, on Redcar Pier and at many private houses throughout the town. The Chairman of the Council despatched the following telegram to the Prince of Wales.

"The inhabitants of Redcar send their heartfelt sympathy on the loss of your beloved mother and our most gracious monarch."

Saturday, the day of the funeral, was observed as a day of mourning throughout the country. All business in Redcar was suspended for the day and most houses had the blinds drawn.

DRAMAS AT SEA

Only a few weeks before Queen Victoria's death, the town had mourned the loss of three brave Redcar fishermen. Early in the morning of 9th January, the steam trawler *Honoraria* of Hull ran ashore at Marske in fog. The coastguard called out Redcar Rocket Brigade and the Saltburn Lifeboat and both went promptly to the rescue. Seven Redcar fishermen heard of the boat's distress. They pushed a coble on its wheels the three miles to Marske to launch it nearer the stricken steamer. Unfortunately, the coble became entangled with the ropes thrown by the Rocket Brigade. Dick Picknett and his sons, Edmund and Jack, were thrown overboard by the rough seas. With the exception of Thomas Hood Picknett, all were drowned. The crew of the trawler were taken off by the Saltburn Lifeboat. In March 1901, the *Redcar and Saltburn News* reported that a monument was to be erected in Redcar Cemetery to the three gallant fishermen who, in trying to save the lives of others, lost their own. The stone, which was erected by public subscription, consists of an anchor looped over a cross.

There was great excitement on 13th November, 1901, when a ship was seen to be in distress off Redcar. The German schooner *Gertrude* was heading for Leith with a cargo of cement. She looked helpless in the heavy seas. The master turned her head to land and in a desperate bid to run ashore, crashed over the rocks. She beached near the bottom of Bath Street. There, amidst cheers, the lifeboat took off the crew of four who were then well cared for in the Queen Hotel.

THE CORONATION OF EDWARD VII

In April 1902, Redcar Council held a special meeting to consider the most fitting way to celebrate the approaching coronation, planned for June. It was decided that the school children would each be presented with a chocolate box bearing a portrait of the king and queen on the lid. Afterwards, the children would sing the National Anthem at Central Square (near the site now occupied by the Town Clock). They would then proceed to the racecourse where they would be given a tea of buns, cake and milk. Later there would be amusements until dusk. On the second day there would be a dinner, in the Central Hall, for the old people who would also be entertained by Mr. Groves' Pierrots. In the evening, there would be a firework display, sports for men and women, and a torchlight procession to round off the night.

In the event, the coronation had to be postponed as the King was seriously ill and the arrangements had to be somewhat modified. The children still received their chocolates and their special tea. The dinner for the old folk went ahead as planned but all the other events were postponed. The coronation festivities were resumed a month later. There was a maypole competition amongst the schools of the district; the first prize of £1 went to Zetland School. Coronation Day was not observed as a holiday in Redcar, although the town was finely decorated with flags and displays. Festivities really got underway on the Bank Holiday Monday. In the afternoon, people crowded on to the pier to watch the regatta. In the evening thousands turned out to watch sports and games in the streets. There were wheelbarrow races, donkey races, 'go-as-you-please' races, a greasy pole competition and a hot rolls-and-treacle competition. After dark, a maypole dance was performed in the school garden at Coatham, followed by a torchlight procession. A large derelict boat was burned on the beach and there were fireworks on the pier. In the early evening, many of the younger people gathered at a large hall in Wilton Street and danced to the Volunteer Band until three o'clock the next morning.

THE KING EDWARD VII MEMORIAL CLOCK

In March 1902, the Council decided to purchase a public clock, to be placed in Central Square, as a celebration of the coronation of Edward VII. The idea did not receive as much support as had been expected and the idea was shelved. Nine years later, the scheme re-emerged, this time as a memorial to the late King.

The structure was completed at the end of 1912. On January 29th, 1913, crowds gathered in Central Square to watch the ceremony of setting the clock in motion. Members of the Council and other eminent gentlemen took the platform adjacent to the new clock. The local Territorials, men of the National Reserve, Boy Scouts and the Church Lads Brigade were positioned around the clock, and Warrenby Band played. Councillor Hudson was presented with a silver knife with which he cut the tri-coloured ribbon holding the pendulum. As the clock was set in motion, the square echoed to the cheers of the crowd. When built, the clock was weight-driven; after the Second World War, it was converted to electricity and a small motor now drives the hands. A bell, weighing 4½cwt. was originally installed to chime the hours. Following complaints from nearby residents, kept awake through the night, the chiming mechanism was disconnected. The bell was removed in 1974 and given to Marske Parish Church; it was melted down and the metal added to the new bells installed there in 1975.

THE GROWTH OF THE TOWN

At the beginning of the twentieth century there was a pressing need for more houses in Redcar. According to the *Redcar and Cleveland News* in 1902:

"If fifty houses were provided, they would be quickly snapped up. Knowing this, it is surprising that the owners of land are so dilatory in opening out new sites for building."

From 1900 till 1914, the town grew rapidly southwards. Five streets were laid between Lord Street and the railway lines and named Muriel, Alfred, Charlotte, Charles Streets and Zetland Place. The majority of the new development was beyond the railway lines, around West Dyke Road.

"West Dyke, or as some call it, 'Klondyke,' is a growing district. There has been a remarkable change in a year. There are now nearly ninety houses occupied on the Redcar side. Some houses are very good ones. Amongst the best are those built by Mr. Hodgson in Hodgson Terrace and West Dyke Road. (Hodgson Terrace is now that part of West Dyke Road between Birdsall Row and the gas depot). Mr. Holder has erected a number of excellent houses. Holder Street and Birdsall Row are superior workmen's houses and when the roads are finished, it will be a very comfortable locality." *Redcar and Saltburn News, April 1901*

Other streets built south of the railway at this time included Soppett, Hanson and Scott streets. Thrush Road was made in 1906, linking West Dyke Road and Redcar Lane. *Observer,* writing in the *Redcar and Saltburn News* in February 1906 described the building work in progress south of Thrush Road.

> "Two houses are in course of erection near Redcar Lane and a great number of cottages are being built near the Race Course. There will be a very large increase of population in this area very soon. The houses erected are mainly for workmen and their families and are a great improvement on this class of building."

The report referred to Lawrence Street, George Street and several others between Thrush Road and Lumley Road. The whole of this area near the racecourse was completed between 1906 and 1910.

On the other side of West Dyke Road, Westfield Terrace was developed between 1910 and 1914. Not to be confused with the Avenue of the same name, Westfield Terrace is now part of Easson Road. Westfield House, Hylton Villa and Mallins Lodge are amongst several imposing villas there. The local newspaper commented further on development in this area in March 1914.

> "As proof of Redcar's growth, it is shown that there are now nearly 550 houses in the West Dyke district alone, and building is still going on there. Not many years ago, there were but 50 houses in West Dyke."

To accommodate the rapidly rising population in this new part of the town, two footbridges were built over the railway lines. The first bridge was built in 1906 by the Railway Company, linking Red Lion Street to Birdsall Row. Two years later, the Council petitioned the Company for a second, at the West Dyke crossing. It was built in 1912. Originally it was intended to give access to the 'Special' platform on busy days. Eventually the Railway Company was persuaded to open the bridge to the public on the understanding that the Company retained the right to close or remove the bridge at any time.

NEW PUBLIC BUILDINGS

A new Roman Catholic Church was needed as the existing building in Thrush Road had become inadequate. The new Church of the Sacred Heart, in Lobster Road, seated about 350 people. It was opened for public worship by the Bishop of Middlesbrough on 17th June, 1914. The old building was later taken over by the Methodist Church.

The first Redcar Literary Institute, erected in 1909 was to be used for meetings, lectures and concerts. It consisted of a hall of corrugated iron, seating 350 people. Public lending libraries were not then established hence an important function of the Literary Institute was the provision of a Reading Room and library for the town.

A better fire-fighting service was needed. In 1910, the Council applied to the Local Goverment Board for sanction to borrow £550 for new fire appliances and for a new Fire Station. After an enquiry, held in the town, permission was granted and the new Fire Station built in Pierson Street. The site has since been redeveloped as the present council's depot for refuse collection vehicles.

THE STRUGGLE FOR A COURT

Until 1910, Redcar had no facilities for the administration of justice; Guisborough was the nearest court. In 1901 Redcar Council first pressed their claim for a petty sessions to be held in the town. The Justices at Guisborough were not sympathetic. From their reply, it appeared that there was insufficient crime in the town to justify an appeal to the County Court for the establishment of a court at Redcar.

In February 1905, at a well attended meeting of magistrates at Guisborough, Mr. John Bulmer proposed, " That a Petty Sessions be held fortnightly at Redcar Urban Council Chamber for the following parishes — Redcar, Coatham, Marske, Saltburn, Wilton and Kirkleatham." Seconding the motion, The Marquess of Zetland spoke of the growth of the Redcar district. All the magistrates voted in favour. Six months elapsed. At a meeting of magistrates at Guisborough, Colonel Locke enquired as to what steps had been taken since February. The chairman replied that he had recently visited Redcar and inspected the premises for the proposed court. Although offered rent free by Redcar Council, they were not suitable for a police court. A new Police Station was erected in France Street in 1908. It was suggested that the fortnightly courts be held there.

In 1909, the magistrates unanimously reaffirmed their belief that Redcar should have a police court. It only remained for the North Riding Standing Committee to confirm the decision and the court could be established. In August, the magistrates met at the new police station and discussed again the establishment of

Petty Sessions at Redcar. It was resolved to use the Inspector's room as a temporary courtroom. The Court House was built eventually, as an annexe to the police station. The first courts were held on the first and third Friday of each month. The Petty Sessions commenced on 21st January, 1910. Sir Alfred Pease presided and twelve magistrates, probably the entire bench, were present at the inauguration. The first case was one of drunkenness on Election Day.

THE SALT WATER SCHEME

The Salt Water Scheme was an important sanitary improvement. It was intended to supply water for dousing the streets and flushing the drains. Redcar is built on the flat coastal plain and the gravity flow through the drains was quite inadequate in parts of the town. Regular flushing of the drains swept away any residual sewage which, if uncleared, would cause blockages. At first there were objections from those who thought that the system was unnecessary. The Council unanimously approved the proposed scheme in 1906 and the work was completed the following year.

HOW REDCAR NEARLY HAD ELECTRICITY!

In 1900, at considerable cost, the Council secured a Provisional Order to supply the town with electricity. However, they did no more about it. As the *Redcar and Saltburn News* so aptly put it:

"They have simply obtained the right to supply electricity and then folded their arms and gone to sleep."

Several years later, they sold the right to make electricity to the Cleveland and Durham Electricity Supply Company. They proceeded no further. In 1910 a second company applied to the Board of Trade to have the Order revoked and to have a second Order made in their favour. The Council was invited to comment on the application. At a special meeting, called to discuss the matter, one council member proposed that the Cleveland Company should be asked to serve electricity within two years; this was seconded. An amendment was proposed and seconded that no action be taken. There were five votes for both the amendment and the motion and the chairman declined to use his casting vote. The matter was left unresolved for a few more years.

The Board of Trade then asked the Council for its observations on the proposal to revoke the Redcar Electric Lighting Order.

The Council decided that it wished to have the Order maintained if the Cleveland and Durham Electric Power Company gave an assurance that the town would be supplied with electricity within two years. This decision was reached in October 1913. Before it could be implemented, World War broke out in 1914 and the plans were shelved.

THE SUFFRAGETTES

The suffragettes brought their campaign to Redcar in the summer of 1909. Miss A. Pankhurst was the chief speaker at an outdoor meeting near the pier on Redcar beach, on Monday, 28th June. The following Thursday, Mrs. Pankhurst herself addressed a large gathering in the Central Hall. Her audience was sympathetic and she was frequently interrupted by applause. Miss Drummond and Miss A. Pankhurst also spoke in the Institute Hall. Mrs. Pankhurst returned to London from Redcar. The station was crowded with friends and sympathisers and loud cheers broke out again and again as the train steamed out of Redcar.

THE CORONATION OF GEORGE V 1911

Redcar entered the Coronation celebrations with gusto. The streets, houses and shops were all decorated with flags and bunting. Residents over 65 years of age were treated to a dinner at which they were waited upon by ladies and gentlemen of the town. The meal was followed by musical entertainment and at the close, the guests were presented with gifts of tea and tobacco. During the afternoon, school children competed in sports on the racecourse. Afterwards, they returned to their schools for afternoon tea and then they each received a box of chocolates and a coronation mug.

Redcar Pier from Steamer Jetty, 1870–1880

Coatham Pier, 1875–1880

Plate 9

Coatham Ironworks, Downey & Co., 1890

Sir Wm. Turner's School (Coatham Grammar School), 1900

Plate 10

Coatham Road, about 1900

Coatham Road, 1st April, 1917   Plate 11

Coatham Enclosure, 1936

Coatham Enclosure Illuminations, 1937-38

Plate 12

CHAPTER TEN
THE SEASIDE RESORT 1900-1914

AT the beginning of the twentieth century, Redcar still maintained its image as a genteel watering place. With increasing mobility, day trippers were becoming a growing class of visitors. The *Redcar and Saltburn News* acknowledged their importance towards the end of the 1903 summer season.

> "The best part of the season is now over at Redcar and it cannot be said to have been prosperous. Certainly a lot of people have been here but they have been largely trippers who certainly are very welcome but one would like to see more permanent visitors who would stay in the town a reasonable time and so benefit Lodging House Keepers and tradesmen to a greater degree."

That Redcar was unprepared for the new type of visitor is clear from the lack of facilities for them. The most urgent need was for public conveniences. In 1901 the *Redcar and Saltburn News* declared it a 'disgrace to a civilised community' that when as many as 25,000 excursionists visited the town in one day, not one public convenience had been provided. The other great need was for shelters in case the weather turned inclement.

> "Is there any place in the world so far behind the times as Redcar? Yet another season bringing its thousands of trippers daily, and no shelter of any kind . . . No wonder the complaints of bad seasons. It would be wonderful if they had a good season."   *The Northern Echo, July 1909*

The town was slow to react to the new demands and two years passed before sheltered seating was erected. There were however, other improvemnts which improved the amenities and changed the face of the resort.

In October 1903, the Surveyor submitted plans for extending the promenade and building a bandstand and lavatories. The Council approved the plans and applied for the necessary permission to borrow the £2,500. The usual Local Government Enquiry followed in December, 1903. There were objections to the proposed site of the lavatories on the sea front but the need for them was obvious and permission was duly granted. The promenade extension was completed in the middle of 1904; the original promenade, an asphalt path between the road and the beach, was flagged over and widened towards the sea. In August it was reported to the Works Committee that the new lavatories had been satisfactorily completed.

THE BANDSTAND

Both Redcar and Coatham Piers had carried Bandstands. Coatham pier was wrecked in 1898 and in the same year, a dropped match burnt out Redcar pierhead with its bandstand. For several years a portable bandstand was used. It was wheeled from a site near the museum housing the lifeboat *Zetland* to a second location near the end of West Terrace and concerts were held at alternate ends of the promenade. Plans for a new permanent bandstand were finally approved and building was completed in 1905 at a cost of £400. It consisted of a semi-circular concrete base jutting out into the beach from the promenade. On top was a dais surmounted by a canopy decorated with wrought ironwork. Inside the concrete base were toilets. In 1910 the base was extended to carry a semi-circle of sheltered seats, at an extra cost of £1,000. A small triangular park had been laid out opposite the original bandstand in 1905. The flower beds were in the shapes of the suits of a deck of cards. The park had become a popular meeting place for nannies wheeling their perambulators and was nicknamed 'Titty-bottle Park' by a popular comedian at the Pierrots.

It was generally agreed that with its new bandstand, Redcar was indeed a fashionable resort, it lacked only a professional band. In August 1902 Redcar Council had applied for an Act of Parliament giving it powers to spend money from the rates on a band for the summer season. The cost of having the Act passed through Parliament would have been £550 and the matter was allowed to rest. Now, with its fine Edwardian bandstand the problem needed urgent attention. A Band Committee was established to collect sufficient funds to pay for the band for the season. In March 1909 it was proposed at a Council Meeting that one penny (1d.) be levied on the rates to provide a band for the coming season. Ever-watchful over the council's spending, the Association of Ratepayers polled the town with the following result:

                For a band ...   1,139
                Against   ...   498

The Council then applied to the Local Government Board for the necessary permission to levy a penny rate for a band. The customary Enquiry was held in the Council Chamber on 16th June, 1909. Mr. Sill presented the case for the Council. He explained that the majority of the ratepayers recently polled were in favour of the proposal and offered the following figures in support of his argument :

Residential visitors for the season ...	6,000
Whitsuntide excursionists	27,000
Weekend (rail) tickets	2,000
Visitors on foot	2,000
Total visitors over the Whit holiday	40,000

No evidence was given against the proposal; the Enquiry had been a brief formality. About a week later, formal approval was received. At once a band was engaged to play every evening on the bandstand for the remainder of the season.

ON THE BEACH

Redcar was then a flourishing resort catering for all kinds of visitors. There were regular band concerts, 'pierrots' on the pier, later on a platform on the beach. There were still bathing machines for hire on the beach. Following a complaint from one bathing machine proprietor, presumably worried about changing customs and consequently falling business, the Council ruled that no sea-bathing would be permitted between West Terrace and Redcar Pier, unless from a bathing machine. Such were the labours of children on the beach that their sandcastles merited a special mention in the press.

"The display of sandcastles is annually becoming more interesting and attractive. A few years ago, such a thing was unknown in Redcar, now it has become a common amusement among the children."

Redcar and Saltburn News, 31st August, 1901

There was considerable controversy over what attractions should be permitted on the beach of Edwardian Redcar. The debate was sparked off in 1904, when the Council allowed a noisy steam roundabout on the beach. As a result of many complaints, a special council meeting was called to decide whether or not steam roundabouts should remain on the beach. There were six votes in favour of the roundabouts, one against and the remainder of the members abstained. There were divided feelings in the chamber; in addition to seeking to provide for the visitors, councillors had to weigh the wishes of the residents against the revenue raised for the Council by letting the sites on the beach.

The Marquess of Zetland had leased the sands to the local authority for many years. His Lordship believed that by his charging only a nominal rent, the local authority would have no need to allow undesirable sideshows on the beach in order to make them pay. By May 1906 there were many in Redcar who wanted the control of the sands to revert to the Lord of the Manor, from the Council. Lodging House keepers on the Esplanade voiced their worries that visitors would not seek accommodation in houses adjacent to noisy sideshows. They threatened to seek an interview with Lord Zetland who, they felt, assuredly would not want his tenants injured in this way. The following season, in July 1907, Lord Zetland gave notice to the Council that he intended to terminate the lease of the sands.

" With reference to the complaints of performances upon the sands at Redcar," His Lordship wrote. " It appears to me necessary that the whole question of erections and performances upon the sands should be carefully considered."

In a letter to the local paper, dated August 1907, *Observer* described the scene on the beach which had brought about Lord Zetland's action.

> " I had a stroll on the Esplanade early one morning and got a fair impression of what the beach looks like when the crowds are not present . . . I counted thirty shanties, more or less undesirable, occupying the best position of a watering place . . . It is not before time that the Lord of the Manor is interfering in this matter. Just for the sake of a few paltry rents, the Council sacrifice the interests of the residents and traders whose welfare is evidently no concern of theirs."

Early in 1908, Mr. Hall, agent for Lord Zetland met the Council at Redcar to discuss the terms for reletting the sands. His Lordship was willing to renew the lease but would exact more stringent regulations so that frontages on the Esplanade would not be "annoyed and injured by unseemly exhibitions" as had occurred in the past. In March, the Council discussed the draft agreement submitted by Lord Zetland. It was proposed and carried that the agreement should not be approved as the Council would be unable to make the sands pay under the conditions as set out. Facilities on the sands changed dramatically from one extreme to the other. In 1907 the beach was thronged with crowds amusing themselves with every conceivable amusement. In 1908 there was nothing. The prohibition had an adverse effect on the town, the day-trippers went elsewhere. Ironically, one party which had visited Redcar for several years went instead to Marske, sea-side home of Lord Zetland.

"1908 has been a year of depression and disaster both nationally and locally. Everyone in Redcar has felt the depression keenly. Visitors were fewer in number and both lodging house keepers and traders suffered materially... The removal of all kinds of attractions from the beach also reduced the number of trippers so that less money was spent in the town in every way."

Redcar and Saltburn News, 1909

Even those who had previously objected to the manner in which the foreshore was managed expressed a desire to see a little brightness and life return. In March 1909 Lord Zetland's agent wrote to the Council offering to lease the beach on the same terms as expressed the previous year. The agent was invited to discuss the matter and in June agreement was reached. The sands would be leased to the Council with certain conditions. A range of attractions, excluding steam roundabouts, would be permitted again. With amusements for visitors restored, the town flourished. As World War approached the popularity of Redcar went from strength to strength.

The new Pier Pavilion, built over the entrance to the defunct Coatham Pier, opened for concert parties in 1910, later it was used for dances too. The Central Hall re-opened in what had been the first railway station, under the direction of the Fenton Picture Company. This new American entertainment quickly proved popular and by 1912 there were three cinemas in Redcar. In 1913 the Palace of Varieties was built on the Esplanade. In 1911 the number of visitors who came to Redcar broke all records. Over 40,000 visitors — four times the town's resident population, poured in on Whit-Monday.

"Redcar is perhaps best described as a homely and wholesome seaside resort with no pretentions to smartness."

Yorkshire Post, August 1911

The beach and Esplanade were not the town's only attractions. Tea gardens and a roller-skating rink had been opened on Redcar Lane and were well patronised. The focus of attention did of course remain on the sea-front. During that last hot summer before the war, Sam Paul's Pierrots were performing on the beach near the remains of the old Coatham Pier; the Waddlers Concert Company, also on the beach, was drawing large crowds. The Palace Pictures mixed its bill with such features as the Brothers St. John Dancers and performing monkeys and dogs. At the Pier Pavilion the Valentines were playing to good houses. The band played four nights each week at the recently extended bandstand in the centre of the promenade. " Redcar for Happy Holidays " was as true then as when it became the town's official slogan two decades later.

CHAPTER ELEVEN — 1914 - 1918
THE FIRST WORLD WAR

WAR was declared on Friday, 14th August, 1914. The next day the Redcar Company of Territorials paraded at the Drill Hall in the High Street and thousands of residents gathered to watch their departure.

"Never in history has Redcar been moved as it was yesterday. With warships hovering near the coast and men getting ready to do service for their country, excitement was raised to fever pitch." *Redcar and Saltburn News*

Early in September, a large number of young men who had already enlisted, left Redcar for their various training quarters. The outbreak of war had an immediate and damaging effect on what remained of the 1914 summer season; Redcar Races were abandoned and all excursions to the town were cancelled. There remained a steady flow of visitors and much of life continued as usual.

"The children are busy building castles in the sand and paddling in the sea, visitors, are sitting on the front and enjoying the sea breezes and there is no indication that anything unsual is taking place."

Redcar and Saltburn News

Throughout the country Recruitment Meetings were held to encourage enlistment. One such meeting, at the Palace of Varieties in Redcar, was so well attended that the auditorium quickly filled and many people were unable to gain admittance.

ON THE HOME FRONT

Shortly after 8 o'clock on the morning of 16th December, Redcar was roused by the sound of heavy firing. Hundreds rushed to the Promenade and saw enemy warships close to the shore. The vivid flashes of shell-fire were quickly followed by an eruption of flames at Hartlepool. The bombardment lasted about forty minutes. Throughout Redcar houses were shaken and windows rattled, yet there was no panic in the town, just a terrible feeling of anguish for the people of Hartlepool. One hundred and twenty-seven were killed, five hundred injured and the town severely damaged.

A later incident, still remembered by older residents of Redcar, occurred on the night of 8th August 1916. A Zeppelin airship dropped bombs on the outskirts of the town, possible aiming for the military camp near Green Lane. No one was killed or injured and very little damage was done. The German airship then headed towards Hartlepool where it was caught in the searchlight beams. A fighter plane took off from Seaton and to the wild cheers of the Redcar onlookers, the huge dirigible was brought down in flames off Hartlepool.

The town celebrated Christmas 1914 very quietly. The Redcar Ironworks band played in the town on Christmas Eve in an attempt to infuse a little Christmas spirit but, with their minds on friends and relatives in the trenches, people at home were subdued. The Redcar Women's Unionist Association forwarded to each Redcar man serving in the Navy or Expeditionary Force, a Christmas present. Each man received a pair of mittens, a pair of socks, a body belt, a scarf, a box of chocolates, a packet of cigarettes and a box of matches, a tablet of soap and a box of foot powder. The Territorials and others in training received a box of chocolates. On Christmas Day, the soldiers stationed in the town each received a small useful gift.

THE " MILITARY " IN TOWN

All over the country, Kitchener's New Army was training. At least three regiments were quartered at Redcar during the course of the war, including the Royal Munster Fusiliers, the 4th South Staffordshire Regiment and the 3rd Battalion the Welsh Regiment. The army had a camp on the racecourse and more troops were billeted in the Pier Pavilion and at Coatham Convalescent Home. West Dyke School was taken over by the military in 1916. Pupils were transferred to Zetland School with each school using the building for half a day at a time alternatively. The soldiers stationed in the town appreciated the hospitality of the people of Redcar. The Lord Mayor of Cork wrote in December 1915, paying tribute to the citizens of Redcar for their kindness towards the Royal Munster Fusiliers during their training in the town.

The spring of 1917 had seen very severe weather, with snow drifts from four to ten feet deep. The troops there at the time had rendered invaluable help with snow clearing. On their departure in June 1917, the Commander, 4th South Staffordshire Regiment wrote : 'We shall carry away very pleasant memories of Redcar, in spite of the severe weather.'

At the beginning of the war, Kirkleatham Hall was transformed into a Red Cross Hospital with thirty-five beds for wounded soldiers, including some from the newly established flying fields at Redcar and Marske. Mrs. Mowbray, housekeeper at the Hall did not enjoy this part of the war. 'The Military were everywhere, and I could not run the house in the proper manner.' In 1917 the hospital was transferred from the Hall to Red Barns, in Coatham.

> "Red Barns, once a gentlemen's residence *(the Bell family, see page 57)* is now a most complete and up to date hospital with 105 beds, an operating theatre, a dining room and a recreation room."
> *The Cleveland Standard*

The military authorities required the beach to be cleared completely each evening so there seemed little likelihood of there being any amusements at all on the beach for the 1915 summer season. The Council applied for modifications to the restrictions, suggesting that moveable stands might be erected between Redcar pier and the remains of the Coatham Pier. This was refused on the grounds that such amusements would draw crowds and lead to damage to the coastal defences. The Council decided to take no further action. It resolved not to grant licences for pleasure boats or donkeys, nor to hire a band for the season. Lord Zetland was approached and asked to consider suspending the lease of the beach for the duration of the war. Despite the absence of the traditional entertainments visitors still came to the town as evidenced by the 'List of Visitors' published as usual in the *Redcar and Saltburn News* from July until September. The situation remained unchanged in 1916. The military authorities regretted that they were still unable to permit amusements on the beach. Despite the constraints of war, Redcar, if not thriving, was surviving.

> "Although the War has been responsible for the considerable falling off of visitors to the seaside resorts, Redcar has had little to complain of in this respect, for during August, no less than 200,000 passengers arrived by train, thus entailing 170 relief trains to convey the holidaymakers home!"
> *Cleveland Standard, September 1916*

During the last year of the war, Redcar recovered its earlier popularity and in August 1918, the attendance records for visitors was again broken.

R.N.A.S. REDCAR

The Royal Naval Air Station was established at Redcar in July 1915; it first appears in Admiralty lists in August 1915. The airfield was established on Low Farm, on land which is now between Roseberry Square shopping centre and the racecourse; it stretched from the boundary of 'Bean's Field' — roughly where Orchard Road is — south almost to the A174 Kirkleatham to Marske road. The first aeroplanes landed on the racecourse and the hangars and accommodation were erected on the farmland during the autumn and winter. In February 1916, the District Surveyor of Coastal Guard Works in York, asked the Council to provide a piped water supply to the camp site. Previously water had been carried from Low Farm.

The Navy had been entrusted with the coastal defence of Britain. In addition to anti-submarine patrols, Redcar was an important training station. In a field near Lazenby there were bombing targets. There was concern about the reliability of the aeroplanes for night flying training.

> 'I should very much like to have Anzani Caudrons for carrying out more extended night flights. The 80 hp. Gnomes are not as reliable for night work and in consequence the risk of forced landings at night would be minimized by Anzani engines.'   *Station Report, 31st July, 1915*

The first aircraft at the station, on 6th July, were a Bleriot XI and a couple of Caudron GIII's. These frail aircraft were sent along the coast 'scouting' for enemy submarines. They were later joined by a flight of four Handley Page 0/400 bombers.

Many aircraft arrived by road and, presumably, by rail. They were erected on the flying field. On the 1st August three more Caudron GIII's and another Bleriot XI were tested and ready. Activity was intense, by November, the station had Bleriot XI's, Caudron GIII's, R.A.F. (Royal Aircraft Factory) BE 2c's, Bristol Scout C's, Curtiss's, Bristol TB8's, Voisin's, and in December there were a couple of Avro 504C's.

Crashes were a regular, almost daily occurence. Although few pilots were killed in their low performance aircraft, the life expectancy of both men and machines was such that a spirit of bravado and adventure quickly built up. Sometimes this overcame the constraints of flying discipline.

'Complaints having been made to the Council, of flying feats by Airmen on Sunday night last, over the Bandstand and houses adjacent, and over crowds of people to the danger of the public.

'Moved Cllr. Metcalf: Seconded Cllr. Spellman. Carried unanimously: That the Clerk be directed to write to the Officer Commanding the Airmen at Redcar, drawing his attention to the danger to the public arising from the above cause and asking him to let exhibitions of flying such as these complained of take place further from the Town and the crowds assembled there.'

Redcar U.D.C. Minutes, 2nd July, 1917

Number 7 Squadron (Naval) flew a flight of Handley Page 0/100 Bombers on operations against submarines in September and October 1917. Eleven U-boats were attacked and seven slightly damaged. In May 1918, 510 flight of 252 Squadron was posted to Redcar to protect shipping around Teesmouth. The flight was disbanded in January 1919 and from then until 1941, Redcar was designated an auxiliary landing ground.

PEACE CELEBRATIONS

On Monday, 11th November, 1918, at 5 a.m., the Armistice was signed. Hostilities were to cease on all fronts at the eleventh hour of the eleventh day of the eleventh month. As soon as the news reached Redcar, the Band of the Welsh Regiment paraded through the town, playing patriotic airs. After lunch, there was a public meeting, held in the open near the Town Clock and presided over by Councillor T. Phillipson. In the evening there was a Thanksgiving Service at St. Peter's church. Most workpeople in the town had a holiday from noon on Monday until Tuesday evening. The streets were thronged with singing, cheering crowds.

July 19th, 1919, was declared to be Peace Saturday. Earlier that month, the Council decided, that with the prospect of heavy financial commitments following the war, it would not draw any expenses from the rates to meet the costs of peace celebrations. The decision was unpopular to say the least. The people of Redcar felt disgraced that they, almost alone in the whole of Cleveland, would not have any public celebrations on Peace Saturday. The Sailors' and Soldiers' Association took the matter in hand and decided to provide a special treat for the children. They planned their celebrations for the following Saturday, the 26th, with a parade and children's sports on the racecourse.

On Thursday evening, 17th July, less than thirty hours before Peace Saturday, Redcar Council reacted to the strong local opinion. At the eleventh hour a programme of events was hastily planned. School children were to assemble at their respective schools at 1 p.m. and march to the Town Clock. After singing the National Anthem, they were to proceed to the Council field and Councillor Spellman's field for sports and games. Tea would be provided for them in West Dyke School. A Donkey Derby was to be held in the evening and there would be other sports in the High Street.

The Council's treat was a huge success and as a result of the 'misunderstanding' of what the townspeople expected of their council, the children were feted twice. Over 2,700 youngsters were entertained the following Saturday by the Ex-servicemen's Association. A great procession was formed on the Promenade. After parading through the main streets, the crowds moved to the racecourse. There were sports, competitions, a baby show and refreshments. Each scholar was presented with a penny and later received an illuminated certificate to celebrate the return of peace. A complete cinematic film was made of the procession by Messrs. Gaumont and Company and later shown at one of Redcar's cinemas.

The peace celebrations were thought to be over then the Council announced that a special banquet would be given in September for all ex-servicemen in the district. During the afternoon, a grand sports display was held on the racecourse. 'Bomb-throwing,' 'blindfold drill' and other competitions provided a great deal of amusement for participants and spectators alike. In the evening about 1,250 ex-servicemen sat down to the banquet at Redcar aerodrome. Local farmers and butchers gave 900 pounds of meat and the tradesmen of the town provided other essentials.

THE MEMORIAL TANK

A German Tank was formally presented to the town, on 15th July 1919, as a memento to the community's patriotic money-raising efforts during the war. Mr. Charles Dorman performed the ceremony, handing over the tank on behalf of the National War Savings Association. The tank arrived by train and was unloaded at the 'Special' platform adjacent to Kirkleatham Street. There was a procession from the station, down Station Road and through the High Street. The day was very hot and the tank made deep ruts in the surface of the road. It was placed at the east end of the High Street, at the junction with the Esplanade, where there is now a paved area. It remained there for some years, a memento for the adults, a plaything for children and a curio for visitors. Towed by two traction engines along Granville Terrace, the tank was later displayed at the end of Lilac Grove, facing the gates of Zetland Park. During the Second World War it was disposed of in a national campaign to provide metal for munitions. With some of the proceeds, two seats were provided on the Lilac Grove site by the British Legion and there is still a commemorative plaque in the gabled wall of the garage on that corner.

THE WAR MEMORIAL

The Council appointed a sub-committee in 1919, to be responsible for providing the town's war memorial. There were insoluble differences of opinion as to the form which the memorial should take and the committee was disbanded.

Six years later, in 1925, the subject was raised again at a Council meeting. As a result, the Mayor and the Aldermen were to call a meeting of citizens of Redcar to discuss raising money to pay for the memorial. Months later, in September of the same year, representatives of the British Legion suggested that it was time positive action was taken over the proposed war memorial. They also offered to support any fund-raising efforts. By then £200 had been raised. It was decided to organise a house-to-house collection. Thus each household would have the opportunity of supporting this tribute from the community.

The War Memorial was unveiled on 6th November, 1926, by Viscount Lascelles, son-in-law of the King. It takes the form of an obelisk in Portland Stone and stands in front of the Municipal Buildings in Coatham Road, Redcar. Strangely, it does not record those lost in the First World War. Their names are displayed in the parish churches, seventy-six names in Christ Church, Coatham, and ninety in St. Peter's, Redcar.

CHAPTER TWELVE — 1918 - 1939

BETWEEN THE WARS

DORMANSTOWN

MESSRS. Dorman Long & Co., had purchased Redcar Ironworks from Messrs. Walker, Maynard & Co. Ltd., early in 1916. They intended having the six furnaces back in full blast during that year. In 1917 Dorman Long had entered into an agreement with the government to increase their production of steel and to this end, they had decided to build a new steel works at Warrenby. The scheme included a 400 ton mixer, ten large steel furnaces, a cogging mill and two large plate mills. It was estimated that between five and six thousand men would be employed when the scheme was completed.

"Redcar's Garden City" is the headline over the first newspaper article about Dormanstown, in the *Cleveland Standard* of 1917. To house the workmen needed to man the new steel works, Dorman Long planned to build a whole new community, on the line of a 'Garden City.' The *Cleveland Standard* reported in December 1920, that there were 76 houses already occupied and another 20 almost ready; 25 houses had been started at the Redcar end of the village and a further 50 were under construction at the west end. For the purposes of local government, a new extension order was issued by the Ministry of Health on 1st October, 1920, to include Dormanstown within the Redcar Urban District.

INCORPORATION

After the First World War, rapid strides were made in the administration of local government. In 1919 Redcar Gas Company offered to sell their works and plant to the Council. Despite public opposition to the transaction, the Council agreed terms and took over the gas works.

Redcar Urban District Council petitioned the County Council for the union of Redcar and Coatham Civil Parishes. Permission was granted in October 1920, thus removing the only remaining legal distinction between the formerly separate villages. More importantly, the formation of the Union of the parishes, gave the town a uniform rating system. The largest change was the extension of the district in 1920. The Extension Order brought

Dormanstown within Redcar Urban District. The population was increased by nearly 2,500 and the acreage of the district was almost doubled. The Council needed more spacious accommodation for its increased staff and responsibilities. "Seafield" in Coatham Road was bought in 1920 and turned into the new Council Offices.

Until the 1850's there had been no local government body at all, only the Poor Law Union which made some provision for those unable to support themselves. In 1855 Redcar Local Board of Health was formed; the prime function was to create a drainage system for the town and then to enforce standards of planning and layout of new houses. The Redcar Board had no jurisdiction over Coatham. The early planning of Coatham was largely in the hands of the main landowners, the Newcomen family. One quarter of a century after Redcar, Coatham formed the Kirkleatham Local Board of Health in 1877. Local Boards of Health were replaced by Urban and Rural District Councils in 1894. Redcar UDC was created, but Coatham and Kirkleatham were administered by Guisborough Rural District Council. In 1899 the districts were revised and Redcar and Coatham were united under the one Redcar Urban District Council.

The town's population had more than doubled in the first two decades of the century. In December 1920 the Town Clerk was instructed to prepare a petition to His Majesty in Council seeking the grant of a Charter of Incorporation to the Urban District of Redcar. In less formal language, the town was seeking the status of a Municipal Borough.

To gauge public opinion, a public meeting was held in the Institute Hall in January 1921. About three hundred people attended and adopted a resolution in favour of incorporation. At Dormanstown, a similar meeting also endorsed the application. The petition included the signatures of nearly all the magistrates and most of the professional people in the town. There was no opposition from inside or outside the district. The application was supported by Dorman Long, the largest ratepayer in the district. Nearly two thousand signatures were collected, about one-eighth of the population, and the petition was lodged in February 1921.

An Official Inquiry was held in Redcar Court House on 4th June, 1921. Redcar's case was presented by the Town Clerk, Mr. Robert McLean. He stated that over the last twenty years, the town's population had doubled and that there was every possibility of it doubling again in the next twenty years. He referred to the recent extension of the boundaries to include the village of Dormanstown. He anticipated that large docks and new industries would be developed along the river frontage. It was with this potential development in view that Redcar was presenting the petition for municipal powers.

The Council contended that, as a town growing in importance, Redcar was well able to justify the application. It had its own gasworks, its own water undertaking, its own fire brigade and a weekly Petty Sessions; the entire foreshore was leased from the Kirkleatham and Zetland Estates. The Town Clerk concluded that, although some emphasis had been placed upon industrial change, Redcar must always continue as a sea-side resort. He described the town as ' the lung of the great industrial population of Tees-side.'

The chairman of the Council, Mr. B. O. Davies, then quoted various statistics relating to the population, rateable value, the Council's activities and finances. He spoke of the general support for the application amongst the people of Redcar. He was convinced that the town had a great future and that incorporation would best equip it to meet its new responsibilities. The Commissioner then inspected the district and promised that he would submit his report to the Privy Council at the earliest possible date.

Less than a year later, on 24th May 1922, the Town Clerk showed to the Council the Charter, granted to Redcar by His Majesty King George V.

As a Corporate Borough, Redcar was able to apply to the College of Heralds for a coat of arms. It was decided that the design should reflect the industries of the town, both modern and traditional. Ships and fishes shared the design with steel ingots and a blast furnace; the motto means " By sea and Iron " (see frontispiece).

INCORPORATION DAY — 9th NOVEMBER, 1922

The ceremonies started at the new Council Offices in Coatham Road. The Charter Mayor, B. O. Davies, J.P., the Charter Town Clerk, R. McClean, J.P., councillors and many leading townspeople walked via Coatham Road and the High Street to St.

Peter's Church, Redcar Lane. The service, at 11 a.m., was taken by the vicar, Revd. B. D. Lloyd Wilson ; the town's flag was laid on the altar and prayers were said for the future endeavours of the Council. The civic party made its way to the Palace Cinema on the Esplanade. Crowds had been gathering for an hour or so and the police had to clear a passage through the throng. Some 1600 people were packed inside and many more spilled across the Esplanade. The theatre curtain was raised a few moments before noon and the theatre vibrated to the cheers. Capt. Snow, mace-bearer, entered and laid the new mace on the table. Councillor Benjamin Owen Davies was nominated and elected Mayor to further cheering. The mayor was robed and there followed a number of speeches. This, the inaugural meeting of Redcar Borough Council was concluded with good-humoured speeches and the new Council and official guests walked in procession to the Coatham Hotel for luncheon.

The afternoon started with the Mayoress "At Home" in the Institute Hall, with over 400 guests. The party then moved to the Kirkleatham end of the new Trunk Road to Grangetown. County Councillor Henry Beresford-Pierse, a guest at the inauguration, declared the road open and was driven through the ribbon in the mayoral car.

Meanwhile, school children enjoyed special 'cinematographic performances' at the local theatres, returning afterwards to their schools for tea. Each child was given a certificate, bearing photographs of the Mayor and Mayoress. The new First Citizen and his lady spent the remainder of the afternoon visiting each of the local schools. In the evening they returned to the Institute Hall for a concert with 550 old people, followed by a substantial tea at Lonsdale's Café. Later that evening there was a Town Whist Drive and Dance at the Pier Pavilion, organised by the Chamber of Trades. The Mayor and Mayoress attended for the distribution of whist prizes and to lead off the dancing. It was nearly midnight when the party returned to the Municipal Buildings. Fifty tons of coal were distributed to the poor of the town as a celebratory gift.

GIFTS TO THE NEW BOROUGH

The Mayoral chain and emblem was the gift of Sir Arthur Dorman, of Messrs. Dorman Long & Co. The directors of Redcar Race Company presented a gold chain for the Mayoress.

Mr. and Mrs. Benjamin O. Davies bought robes for the aldermen and defrayed the cost of the Coat of Arms. Col. T. W. S. Locke, J.P. presented the mace and Mr. and Mrs. A. O. Cochrane gave the Mayoral and Town Clerk's gowns.

The Marquess and Marchioness of Zetland wired hearty congratulations, and the best wishes of the City of London were sent by its Lord Mayor. Amongst other telegrams were good wishes from the Mayors of Middlesbrough, Thornaby, Darlington, Richmond and Ripon.

UNEMPLOYMENT

Redcar's Incorporation came at the time when the town was suffering the effects of several months of trade depression. This was only the start of the long unbroken period of low employment which affected the whole country. Distressed areas were entitled to receive grants from the Government, the money being used to pay wages to men, otherwise without work, who worked on local schemes. Early in 1921 the Town Clerk had applied for such a grant but it had been denied on the grounds that the problem in Redcar was not yet too serious. The Town Clerk continued to press the Minister of Labour and the Unemployment Grants Committee for a contribution to the schemes which the Corporation were prepared to carry out, if such support was forthcoming.

Several months later, the Minister of Labour conceded that Redcar was an area with a serious unemployment problem and the necessary certification was passed to the Unemployment Grants Committee. The Corporation also had an arrangement with the Board of Guardians under which able bodied men were given work in return for payment from the rates. This scheme was started in 1921 and continued throughout the 1920's. Redcar was the first town in the north to introduce such a scheme and it was copied by other towns throughout the country.

The first scheme was to make a new road to Dormanstown, to replace the narrow country lane, on which there had been frequent accidents. The Unemployment Grants Committee offered to meet 60% of the wages bill. Other schemes included the remodelling of the sewage system, laying electric cables and renewing gas and water mains. The sanitation of the town was greatly improved during this period.

In December 1920, there still remained 87 privies and over 2,000 pail closets in the district. This far exceeded the number of water closets. Ashpit privies were, as the name implies, a convenience where the seat is over a large pit, the contents are covered with ash from time to time and allowed to drain away and decompose into the ground beneath. The pail closet was usually situated against an outside wall of the dwelling. Beneath the seat was a large receptacle which hung on the inside of a hinged door. Sewage was removed during the night, hence the term "night soil," through the hinged trap which opened into the back street.

Between November 1923 and the Spring of 1924, the Corporation made arrangements for the conversion of one thousand lavatories. In September 1924, the Unemployment Grants Committee agreed to fund the completion of the conversion scheme. The remaining work was carried out as an unemployment relief scheme and by the end of the year, the entire town was connected to water carriage system.

THE TRUNK ROAD

Redcar was the nearest and most popular resort for the industrial towns along the Tees. Yet there was no direct route to the coast, only tracks and lanes linking the farms. Traffic from Middlesbrough passed through Lazenby, Normanby and Ormesby. In October 1921 it was decided to build a road between Redcar and Grangetown as part of the proposed Trunk Road to Middlesbrough. Work began in November 1921. The Town Clerk was instructed to employ as many men as possible from the Relief List of the Board of Guardians. By the time it was completed, over 10,000 men had worked on the scheme, over £30,000 had been paid in wages and about 65,000 tons of material had been used. When he officially opened the road, Sir Henry Beresford-Pierse declared that 'This great highway could not fail to add to the town's prosperity.'

CORPORATION ROAD

At the same time as planning the Trunk Road, the Corporation decided to extend the new road from the corner of Kirkleatham Lane to the race course. The Town Clerk enquired of the agent for the Kirkleatham Estate as to the terms under which the Corporation might acquire the necessary land. The Estate made a gift of two acres of land for the road and as a bonus, allowed the Corporation to take such slag from the Estate tips, as was needed for the foundations. In return the Borough was to erect and maintain a fence on both sides of the new road and to provide new gates.

COAST ROAD

The Ministry of Transport offered to the Corporation, in October 1922, a grant equal to half the cost of their section of the proposed new Coast Road to Marske. Until this time, the only route to Marske was either along the sands, or via Redcar Lane (then Church Lane) entering Marske by Redcar Road. Redcar Corporation was to be responsible for the new road from Granville Terrace to the eastern boundary of the town. Marske was administered by Guisborough Rural Council who were responsible for the remainder. Redcar offered to supply Guisborough with slag from tips worked by the Council for 7s. 6d. (37½ pence) per ton, delivered by the Council's private railway to Green Lane. This railway was almost certainly the remains of the mineral track which ran from Coatham junction to New Marske ironstone mines. The Marquess of Zetland was invited to perform the opening ceremony on 9th November, 1923.

A TIME OF IMPROVEMENTS

Existing roads within the Borough were improved as part of the Council's efforts to reduce unemployment. Redcar Lane was widened and resurfaced. West Dyke Road was reconstructed and the Dyke itself covered over and culverted. Public works carried out by the unemployed did much to make the town more attractive. The sandbanks were levelled and the famous Stray was created in 1923. The promenade was extended from "Touchwood" at the end of Granville Terrace. Three new parks were laid out.

A scheme to lay out a recreation ground adjacent to Redcar Lane was approved in October 1923. Borough Park, as it was to be called was chiefly devoted to sport, with football and cricket pitches. Several years later another grant was used to provide fifteen hard tennis courts and a sports pavilion.

Lord Zetland gave six acres of land, near to the junction of Granville Terrace and the new Coast Road. In October 1923 the Council approved plans to turn this into Zetland Park. Work began in January and the park opened to the public the following

June. Semi-circular in shape, it centred round a stream which flowed through a lily pond. There were tennis courts, flowered banks, shrubberies and a beautiful rose walk. The Mayoress, Mrs. B. O. Davies, formally opened the park in June 1924, in the absence of the Marchioness of Zetland who was unable to travel north for the occasion.

THE LOCKE MEMORIAL PARK

Colonel T. W. S. Locke, J.P. was born in 1830 and came to Redcar shortly after the Crimean War. He commenced practice as a doctor; following his profession for over half a century. In 1898 he was appointed a County Magistrate and for twenty-six years he carried out his duties zealously. It was largely due to his interest and support that Redcar had eventually been provided with the Court Building in which the Petty Sessions were held. One of the oldest residents in Redcar, he held offices in several clubs and other organisations in the town. He was vice-chairman of the Literary Institute and a director of the Redcar Pier Company. Colonel Locke was one of the small band of pioneers who formed the Redcar Race Company, he rarely missed a meeting and was a familiar figure in the Stewards stand. He also had an interest in Redcar Cricket Club. He died in Coatham on 21st February, 1924, aged 94.

In his will he left to the Corporation some twenty acres of land with instructions that it should be laid out as a park. For nearly two years the land awaited development. In 1926 the General Strike resulted in many more men losing their jobs. The Council then prepared a scheme to develop Locke Park, as it was to be known, in order to relieve the rising unemployment in the Borough. The following year, in view of the large number of men compelled to seek relief from the Guardians, it was decided to create a lake from the stream which runs through the park. In Autumn 1928, still faced with serious unemployment, the Corporation looked for ways of absorbing the maximum numbers of unskilled men. Further development of the park was deemed an ideal solution. At least 90% of the costs of such a scheme would be dispersed in wages and a substantial grant was received from the government. Further work was done in the Winter of 1929. The park was opened by Mrs. B. O. Davies, in June 1930. After the customary speeches, the good lady was taken for a row round the lake.

The state aided programme not only provided the town with three parks but also with two playing fields for children and the miniature Lily park on the Coast Road estate. It was also to provide further benefits for the flourishing sea-side resort. In 1929 the most ambitious scheme yet was drawn up for the winter months. It was proposed to build a boating lake, bathing pool and indoor swimming baths in the Coatham Enclosure. After holding an inquiry in the town, the Minister of Health gave his approval for the Council to proceed.

The boating lake was to be finished by Easter 1930 and the open air swimming pool a few weeks later at Whitsuntide. The indoor swimming baths were opened in September of the same year. In the early 1950's the open-air pool was converted to a roller-skating rink — ' Redcar's Rollerdrome ' and twenty years later, the site was completely cleared, leaving a grassy hollow in front of the covered swimming baths. The original baths were demolished in 1978 and a new building opened on the same site, built over the original pool, in 1979. Late in 1930 a bathing pool for children was built on the south side of the covered baths. This has long since vanished and is now beneath the car park of the modern baths.

Another unemployment scheme was the building of the road subway at Redcar East Halt railway station ; this scheme was approved in November 1930.

At this time the unemployment problem was growing still more serious. In November 1930 the County Council accepted a proposal to widen the Grangetown section of the Trunk Road to provide relief work for the unemployed. With over 900 men without work in Redcar it agreed to carry the new work through to Redcar, to the junction with Kirkleatham Lane.

This was to be one of the last of the state aided schemes ; by 1931 grants were no longer available. Throughout the country, unemployment figures continued to rise, reaching their peak in 1933. In January of that year, there were over 2,000 people without work in Redcar.

At the beginning of 1934 there were brighter prospects ahead, with signs of an industrial revival in Cleveland. Dorman Long & Co., were planning to restart two blast furnaces to meet the increasing need for pig iron. Men were soon back at work preparing to restart the coke ovens at Warrenby.

CHAPTER THIRTEEN
HOUSING DEVELOPMENT

THE interruption of house-building during the war and its slow revival afterwards caused, by 1921, a severe shortage of housing throughout the country. In Redcar, no houses were built during the war, nor during the following two years. Many families lived in deplorable conditions in 1921. There were three families in some small houses and families even lived under canvas. In July 1919, the Sanitary Inspector and the Medical Officer of Health visited a camp of homeless people in Redcar. They estimated that about 500 were living in tents. The sanitary arrangements were not only inadequate, they were indecent. For the men there were two seats in a shed with a door and two more in a shed without a door. For the women there was a very small shed with one seat and in an adjoining field there were two seats — no mention of a shed! The cookhouse was dirty and ill-ventilated. The owner of the field was given seven days in which to close the site until proper toilets were installed.

TEMPORARY DWELLINGS

In the face of the acute housing shortage, the Council had reluctantly to permit the occupation of temporary dwellings. At best they could try to maintain certain minimum standards. They resolved that plans of temporary buildings would have to be submitted for approval; if they met with the specified standards, approval would be given for twelve months when the buildings would be inspected before the permission was extended.

A plan to erect eight wooden huts in a field off West Dyke Road was approved by the Council in September 1919. The Surveyor made the following report when the huts were completed. Four of the huts had been occupied before a certificate had been issued. One hut had not a lavatory; water was not piped to any of the huts. The windows were not glazed, the frames being covered with cardboard. During the next two years, temporary dwellings were erected on two main sites — in a field off West Dyke Road, now Brooksbank Avenue, and adjacent to Redcar Lane, now St. Peter's Grove. As well as wooden huts, there were caravans and disused railway carriages converted into temporary homes. In June 1920, the *Cleveland Standard* reported that a 'unique auction' would take place that month, when a railway carriage 'recently converted into a desirable residence' would be sold to the highest bidder.

From the number of plans passed by the Council, there were about fifty such temporary homes, but including those built before the Council enforced its planning rules and some which were built without permission, the total may have been nearer seventy.

The first closing order for a temporary dwelling was issued in December 1923 when 'Huntcliffe View,' a hut in St. Peter's Grove was described as being unfit for occupation. In June of the following year, the Sanitary Inspector issued a notice to the owner of the Smith Street Camp Field requiring him to clear the field of temporary dwellings. A month later, the Medical Officer was asked to report on such huts as, in his opinion, were unfit for human habitation and should be closed. On his advice, the Council issued closing orders on six huts in Brooksbank Avenue. More huts were closed in the ensuing months.

That same summer, the Town Clerk was instructed to inform the owners of temporary dwellings that all temporary planning certificates would expire in July 1924 and that the Council could not guarantee that permission for temporary buildings would be renewed for a further twelve months. At the same time the Town Clerk pointed out the attractive terms offered to those wishing to replace their huts with permanent houses. The Council was given permission in February 1925, to borrow £5,000. This would provide fifty subsidies of £100 each to the owners of wooden huts who were prepared to erect brick or stone dwellings in their place. The idea was a success and a number of applications were received for the grants. Between 1928 and 1930, the remaining huts in Brooksbank Avenue were cleared; the occupiers were allocated new council houses in Dormanstown. The last demolition order on a temporary dwelling, a hut at 5 St. Peter's Grove, was issued early in 1932.

Even before that, in June 1926, the Medical Officer was confident that the problem was beaten. He reported, 'The vigorous housing policy pursued by the Corporation has abolished any general overcrowding.'

REDCAR'S FIRST COUNCIL HOUSES

A housing scheme based on financial assistance from the Local Government Board was adopted by Redcar Council in November 1918. A committee was appointed to inspect and report on land suitable for such housing. In June 1920 the Council purchased land off West Dyke Road from the Kirkleatham Estate. The Minister of Health sanctioned the borrowing of £14,000 for the erecton of twenty houses. The first council houses were built in Westfield Avenue and were completed by the end of October 1921.

The Council had intended building a further twenty houses in Westfield Avenue but the Minister of Health could not permit them to proceed. The assisted scheme was proving extremely costly and the government was compelled to retract it. A limit was set on the number of houses eligible for assistance. A deputation was sent from Redcar to the Ministry of Health in July 1922. As a result the Council were permitted to build six more houses under the assisted scheme. These were finished in May 1923. The twenty-six houses in Westfield Avenue had been built under the 1919 Housing Act which had proved rather too generous in its terms. Later Housing Acts were so designed as to safeguard the Treasury.

There remained the question of what to do with the remaining land on the Westfield Estate. Eventually the Council sold it to a private builder with certain conditions attached. It was stipulated, amongst other things, that the original layout was to be adhered to and that not more than forty-four houses should be built on the site.

The Government's solution to the housing shortage was to encourage both private builders and local authorities by offering subsidies. This policy, introduced after the first World War continued throughout the 1920's and was withdrawn in the early 1930's.

LOCAL AUTHORITY BUILDING 1923–29

"Above all, this has been a year of housing activity. Last October, we had just accepted a contract for twenty cottages, today work is in progress for providing 251 houses to be let by the Council."

Benjamin Owen Davies, Mayor of Redcar, October 1924

In 1923 and 1924, council houses were built at Dormanstown on Broadway East, Abercrombie Road and Adshead Road. Two adjacent sites were used in Redcar, East of Redcar Lane ; the Lord Street Estate included Beech Avenue, Elm Road and Maple Court ; the Park Avenue development consisted of Park Avenue,

Laburnum Road, Cedar Grove and Lime Road. It was estimated that at weekly rents of 10s. 6d. (52½p) and 12s. 6d. (62½p) and 15s. 0d. (75p), these houses could be let without loss to the Corporation. Before long, the Council was forced to seek ways of cutting its capital commitments.

From 1925, it became the Corporation's policy to encourage the tenants to buy the homes which they occupied, by offering them comparatively easy terms. The tenants were offered 'kitchen houses' at prices from £320 and 'parlour houses' from £400 to £450. Some tenants did not have sufficient savings to put down the necessary deposit. Robert McClean, Town Clerk, proposed an ingenious solution to the problem. He devised a scheme through which those tenants who could not find the deposit were given the opportunity, by weekly contributions, to accumulate an amount sufficient to enable them to approach a conventional building society. This scheme, introduced by Redcar Borough Council was to be copied by many other towns throughout the country.

Local authority building fluctuated between the two World Wars. In Redcar the peak years were 1923-24, 1929-31 and 1935-39. Between 1929 and 1931 development was concentrated at Dormanstown; it appears that Messrs. Dorman Long were selling land for housing at reasonable prices. In 1929 attention was called to the shortage of workmen's dwellings. The Borough Engineer was instructed to prepare plans for sixty council built houses at Dormanstown. These were to be 'kitchen houses,' cheap enough to be let at low rents; on completion, the weekly rent was fixed at 6s. 0d. (30p).

During the next two years, 290 houses were built in Dormanstown with the approval of the Ministry of Health. In February 1932 the Council formally thanked the Directors of Dorman Long & Company for their ready co-operation with the Council's Dormanstown housing schemes which it was claimed, provided dwellings at the lowest overall price for any urban area.

The Rivers Estate, off Kirkleatham Lane, was planned in 1935 but its development and completion was interrupted by the Second World War.

THE PRIVATE SECTOR

The Housing Act of 1923 provided subsidies of £75 per house to which Redcar Borough Council added a further £5. Redcar was able to set an example to other towns, being the first Council to encourage house building by offering the private builder free building sites as an alternative to the lump sum subsidies. This scheme proved remarkably successful and was an important factor in the development of the town.

In February 1925 the Borough Engineer was instructed to plan the layout of the Crescent and the adjacent roads, named after trees, on land which the Council had purchased east of Zetland Park. The following year, the Council bought more land from Lord Zetland to extend the Crescent Estate eastwards. 1929 saw the completion of the 360 sites planned for that year.

The Marquess of Zetland offered forty acres of land to the Council in October 1928. It was to provide housing, between the Crescent Estate and the eastern boundary of Redcar. The purchase was authorised by the Ministry of Health and building commenced on the Coast Road development. First, Cypress, Chester, Laurel and Zetland Roads were built. The Council recommended that the remaining roads in this area should be named after cathedral cities, thus creating Canterbury Road, Ely Crescent and Wells Grove and their environs. The town was fully developed, as far as its eastern boundary by the end of 1935.

The land south of the railway line was developed, largely by the Zetland Estate Company, from 1943 onwards. The roads in this area were named after castles, such as Warwick, Richmond and Stirling.

In 1935, Messrs. Dorman Long submitted a plan for the layout of the Spring Gardens Estate. Approval was given for the roads to be named after local places, including Boulby and Staithes Roads and Kettleness Avenue. Spring Gardens Estate was completed by other private developers in the 1950's.

Early in 1936, the Town Clerk reported that land in West Dyke, then used as a pleasure park, had been sold. The new owner of the pleasure park proposed building a housing estate on the site consisting of Sandringham and Buckingham Roads.

HOMES FOR AGED

Redcar was the first local authority in England to build homes for its senior citizens. The first group of homes, opened in May 1931, were the Sir Arthur Dorman Memorial Homes at Dormanstown. These twenty old peoples' bungalows were built alongside Broadway East on land given by Messrs. Dorman Long. They have the distinction of being the first homes of their kind in the whole country. A week later, the Marquess of Zetland opened the second group of homes for old people, built by the Council. These twenty-four bungalows were built on land given by Lord Zetland in Laburnum Road. In his speech, his Lordship congratulated Redcar Corporation on being pioneers in this field.

" It is a great feather in their caps, that they were the first to take advantage of the legislation passed last year to erect homes for aged people at a reasonable rent."

The rent for the old people's accommodation was fixed at 4s. 11d. (24½p) per week, made up of 3s. 6d. rent and the balance towards local rates. The next phase comprised twelve cottages for old people, erected at Warrenby under the Council's scheme. The Dowager Lady Zetland opened the fourth group of homes for the aged, the Lillian Zetland Homes at Redcar East, in July 1933. Government subsidies ended in 1932. From then on, the building of old people's homes was to be unassisted. In July 1934, the Public Works Loans Commission granted the Corporation a loan of £5,000 for the provision of more old people's homes. Twenty-six homes were built in Dormanstown and the road named after Robert McClean, the late Town Clerk. There were then ninety-six such dwellings in the district.

The most ambitious scheme was prepared in 1937. Forty-six homes were planned for the newly started Rivers Estate and they would be named the Alderman B. O. Davies Memorial Cottages, the first Mayor of Redcar, better known now as Severn Road.

CHANGES IN STREET NAMES

The inter-war period had seen very rapid development of the town. In 1938 it was calculated that more than 60% of the houses in Redcar were built between 1921 and 1939.

DWELLINGS IN THE BOROUGH
1922   —   3,238
1938   —   7,012

During this period a number of streets and terraces were renamed in order to reduce the confusion caused by the similarity of some names which occurred in both Redcar and Coatham, and the difficulty encountered by visitors when one straight road consisted of several differently named terraces. In January 1934, the Plans and Streets Committee suggested the following changes.

EXISTING NAME	PROPOSED NEW NAME
High Street, Redcar	High Street East
High Street, Coatham	High Street West
Zetland Place	France Street
West End West Terrace	West Dyke Road
Cleveland Terrace, Redcar Arthur Place	Railway Terrace
Newcomen Street	Station Road
Wilton Place	Albert Street
Albert Place	Bank Street
Portland Terrace Victoria Terrace Cleveland Terrace Bentinck Terrace Vansittart Terrace Theresa Terrace	Coatham Road
Church Street Railway Cottages George Terrace Cambridge Terrace	Redcar Lane
Broadway East Sandy Lane	Broadway East (changed 1936)

Except as noted, the above changes were made in 1935. A number of other changes were made at the request of residents, in the years indicated.

FORMER NAME	NEW NAME AND YEAR OF CHANGE
Smith Street	William Street (1926)
Hearse Grove	Stanley Grove (1928)
German Street	Bank Street (1932)
Daisy Road	Windsor Road (1935)
Pansy Road	Conway Road (1935)

CHAPTER FOURTEEN

MARKETS

ALTHOUGH a market existed in Redcar during the middle ages, it did not survive through the centuries. The nineteenth century directories make no mention of a market in the town. Not until the twentieth century was market trading revived.

Over three hundred property owners and ratepayers petitioned the Council in December 1921, urging the Council to take the necessary steps to provide a market again. A public meeting was called in January 1922. It was revealed that a large number of Redcar people were travelling to South Bank, Middlesbrough and Stockton in order to shop at the markets there. Perhaps it was the changing character of the town which had generated the need for a market : who, in the nineteenth century could have imagined the gentry of Coatham shopping in a market place ?

> "What was once a middle class business centre has rapidly acquired an equally important clientele of weekly wage earners."
> *North East Daily Gazette*

Since the First World War, Redcar had become more definitely an annexe to industrial Tees-side. The population of Warrenby and Dormanstown was almost entirely working class and the middle class shopping facilities of Redcar did not fully meet their needs. It was decided unanimously at the public meeting to establish a market at Redcar.

The market started on the last Saturday in February 1922 with about fifty stalls ranged along the north side of the broad High Street. In 1927, Redcar Corporation started a second market in Portland Terrace, West Dyke Road. In 1933–34 the two markets brought the Council over £500 in rent from stallholders. After the War, the popularity of the markets declined. In 1951 the High Street market was closed and the stalls transferred to the remaining site in Portland Terrace, opposite the Pig and Whistle in West Dyke Road. This market ceased trading in 1956, despite offers by the remaining stallholders to attend to their own cleaning up. Since 1972 there had been a Sunday Market on Redcar Racecourse. This venture foundered in 1973 due to Sunday Trading Restrictions. It was quickly re-established in the same year and remains very popular to this day.

ACQUISITION OF THE FORESHORE RIGHTS

The Corporation was eager to acquire the foreshore rights within the new Borough. In January 1923, the Town Clerk wrote to the agents of the Zetland and Kirkleatham Estates and enquired about purchasing the foreshore rights. The Zetland Estate replied that Lord Zetland would be advised to sell to the Corporation such rights as he possessed in the foreshore within the Borough for the sum of £2,000. The price was to include the sandbanks north of the new Coast Road. The Council accepted his offer. Certain conditions were included in the conveyance of the foreshore and sandbanks. It was stipulated that no steam organ or other similar noisy instrument should be allowed upon the said land and foreshore. The Corporation also accepted an offer made by the owner of the Kirkleatham Estate to sell his foreshore rights, and the Crown Rights acquired by him in Coatham Foreshore, for the sum of £1,393. Application was then made to the Minister of Health for permission to borrow the sum needed to cover the purchase of these rights.

ELECTRICITY SUPPLIED TO REDCAR — AT LAST!

Electricity, first discussed in 1900, was eventually introduced to Redcar in 1924. In January 1923, the representatives of the Cleveland and South Durham Electric Power Company were invited by the Council to attend a meeting to discuss providing electric lighting for the Borough. The company promised to give the Council a rough estimate of the cost of laying electricity mains in the principal thoroughfares in the town. In October 1923 the Council applied to the Electricity Commissioners for a special order enabling them to supply, distribute and sell electricity within the Borough of Redcar.

The first supplies of electric cable arrived at the end of March 1924. The Borough Engineer fixed piece rate terms with the local unemployed for laying the cable.

The lamps on the Promenade were the first to be lighted. The general scheme for lighting the town was to start a week later on 9th August 1924. More cable was purchased so that electric lighting may be extended to Redcar Lane and other parts of West Dyke. The electric lights were officially switched on at Redcar on 1st September 1924. The inauguration ceremony was performed in the Mayor's Parlour, at the Municipal Buildings, by the Mayoress, Mrs. B. O. Davies.

THE NEW ISOLATION HOSPITAL

The old Fever Hospital near Warrenby was inspected in 1919. The Surveyor found the building very dilapidated, almost uninhabitable. In wet weather it was almost impossible to stem the flow of dripping rainwater. The mattresses were rotten and the bed linen in rags. The Surveyor concluded that the old isolation hospital was 'a standing disgrace to the town.'

The new isolation hospital, at Grewgrass Farm south of Redcar Lane, was opened on 27th July, 1925, by the Mayoress Mrs. B. O. Davies and members of the Corporation. Alderman Spellman, who presided at the opening ceremony, said that for thirty years or more, the question of a joint hospital for Cleveland had been discussed. Redcar was in sympathy with the proposal but they had been unable to get other neighbouring authorities to agree with their proposals. Redcar wanted better hospital accommodation at an early date and, in order to cope with the Borough's development, it was necessary to proceed alone with the present scheme. He explained that the hospital had cost £2,300 but as only £900 had been borrowed, it would not be a burden on the rates. The building, erected under the supervision of the Borough Engineer, had sixteen beds, two observation wards and accommodation for the staff.

NEW SCHOOL AT DORMANSTOWN

In 1922 the Council gave their support to a petition raised in Dormanstown for a new school to replace the existing one in its temporary buildings. Four years later, in May 1926 the new permanent school was opened by Clara Lady Dorman. There was accommodation for over 400 children. In a brief address, Lady Dorman expressed her great pleasure that Dormanstown should at last have 'such a finely designed school.' She spoke warmly to the children. 'I have never,' she declared, 'seen healthier and bonnier children anywhere.'

ALL SAINTS' CHURCH, DORMANSTOWN

For many years, the Parish of Dormanstown had struggled to provide a church for its people. It was not until 1932 that the aspirations of the parishioners were realised and a spacious new church was opened.

When Dormanstown was created, the Archbishop of York immediately appointed a Priest in-Charge to care for the spiritual welfare of the people. The first services were held in the Parsonage; the total collection for the first day was 4s. 11d. (24½p). Later services were held in a small school room and then in a barn and finally in the village hall. This latter arrangement was not satisfactory as the same hall was used as a dance hall and a cinema known as the Majestic but popularly called the 'Bug and Flea.'

Steps were taken to make Dormanstown a separate parish with its own incumbent in 1926. This was accomplished the following year when an Order of Council was issued making Dormanstown a separate ecclesiastical district. That same year, Messrs. Dorman Long & Co., generously gave the village three acres of land for a church and vicarage.

The need for a proper place of worship had become more pressing as the population increased. For years every possible effort had been concentrated on the building fund which, by 1932, had reached over £5,000. Some grants were received but most of the sum had been raised by the people of Dormanstown. Apart from bazaars, it had nearly all been raised by direct giving. By the Spring of 1932, the new church in South Avenue was almost completed and All Saints' Church was consecrated on 28th May, 1932, by the Archbishop of York. The design was a popular one with the church of England and is identical to St. Oswald's Church in Middlesbrough. Should it ever be required, archways can be opened in the south wall and a south aisle added to increase the church's capacity.

THE STEAD MEMORIAL HOSPITAL

Mr. F. Arnold Stead gave his home to the people of Redcar in 1929, to be used as a cottage hospital. The gift was made as a memorial to his father. The late Dr. J. E. Stead, the distinguished metallurgist, had been one of the town's most prominent citizens.

The Local Hospital Charities Committee played a vital rôle in raising funds to equip the new hospital. They provided £500 for furnishing the building and a further 100 guineas for sun-ray apparatus. They also promised £250 towards the upkeep of the hospital during the first year. All the doctors in the town offered their services to the hospital free of charge during the first year. The Doctor Stead Memorial Hospital was formally opened on 26th July, 1929, by the Dowager Marchioness of Zetland. The town's task was then to raise, year by year, the money required to maintain the new hospital. Legacies, flag days and garden parties all helped the hospital pay its way. One of the most successful fund raising efforts was the annual Redcar Charity Ball, held every January in the Pier Ballroom.

Patients were referred to the hospital by the town's doctors. Many, because of their circumstances, received free treatment but those who were able to pay were charged a modest sum per week. At first the facilities were simple. There were only seven beds when the hospital opened. Later two villas, on either side of the original bulding were bought thus increasing the hospital's capacity and extending its facilities. The 'Stead' was renowned for physiotherapy and sun-ray treatment. Minor surgery was carried out at the hospital originally but as the years passed, fewer operations were performed.

Today, the hospital, with over fifty beds, takes patients awaiting surgery at Hemlington Hospital and there are geriatric wards and an outpatients clinic.

REDCAR LIBRARY

The earliest recorded library in Redcar was opened in the Zetland Rooms, in 1848, by Mr. John Harrison, who lent books and magazines from his own collection. From 1898 the Literary Institute provided Library facilities in Redcar. Its library was well patronised but, in later years, it was unable to supply the needs of such a rapidly expanding population.

It was in December 1929 that the Council was first urged to provide free library facilities in Redcar. They enquired as to whether a branch of the County Library might be established in the town. The County Librarian and the Clerk to the Education Committee were invited to a meeting in January 1930 to discuss the matter. The outcome of the meeting was a decision to postpone any decision for several months. Several years elapsed and nothing was accomplished. Then, early in 1933, a deputation was sent to Northallerton to ask again if the County Library Service could be extended to Redcar. The County Education Committee replied, explaining that owing to the current financial situation, the matter would have to be deferred for a further twelve months. After allowing the year to pass, the Council applied again, only to be told that the County Education Committee had once again decided to defer the matter.

Finally, in 1935, the Council appointed a sub-committee to interview the County Library Committee and report back with proposals for establishing a branch library. The sub-committee was then instructed to investigate the possibility of the town providing its own library. The sub-committee concluded that the town could provide its own library slightly cheaper than by using the County service. They could provide the same facilities with the added advantage that the running of the library would be under the control of the Borough Council, not the County authority.

The Libraries Act was then adopted in the town and a Library Committee was appointed. A grant for the provision of books was made by the Carnegie Trust. The ground floor of Ridley House was selected as the most suitable place to house the new library. The Archbishop of York, President of the Library Library Association, opened the library on 8th December, 1937. The enthusiasm of the people of Redcar was overwhelming to the point of embarrasment. The Borough Librarian reported after the first month :

> "The empty shelves in the library can alone show the desparate need for further considerable additions to the bookshelves."

Later the library was extended with a reading room, in an annexe at the rear and a children's section. When the new library was built, on the site of the old Sir William Turner's Grammar School, in 1963, Ridley House was demolished. In its place now stands the B. O. Davies Health Centre.

" REDCAR FOR HAPPY HOLIDAYS "

The town reached its peak as a seaside resort in the years between the two World Wars. After Redcar had become a Borough, the new Corporation spent much time and money advertising the town all over the country. In December 1922, the Council first approved a scheme for advertising Redcar and they voted to spend £200 from the profits made on the beach to this end. A joint advertising campaign with the railway company appears to have had excellent results.

> "We can congratulate the town on its continued progress and upon an extension of its popularity amongst holidaymakers, particularly from the West Riding. The feature of

the past season has been the large increase in the number of people visiting Redcar for the first time."

William Metcalfe, Mayor, in his Annual Review 1926

After the First World War, the bathing machines did not reappear. The Council gave permission for twenty-four bathing tents to be erected on the beach in the Summer of 1921. To protect the interests of the owner of the tents who hired them daily, and thus protect the Council's income from site rent, a local by-law prohibited bathing, other than from these tents between Coatham pier's remains and Granville Terrace. The fixed rate for using the bathing tents was sixpence (2½p) for adults and threepence for children.

The regulation of the beach was originally the business of the General Purposes Committee, later a special Sands and Entertainment Committee was formed. Arrangements recommended by the General Purposes Committee for the 1925 season included:

1. No steam roundabouts should be allowed on the beach.
2. The Corporation should undertake to provide kiosks and the following stalls for the summer: four ice cream, two each for sweets and novelties, and one each for fruit and newspapers.
3. The cloakrooms under the Bandstand should be used for the sale of tea and coffee.
4. Two sets of juvenile roundabouts and two sets of swings should be allowed on the beach.

The Council was determined that the beach should be lively, with plenty of attractions without being too noisy. The contretemps with Lord Zetland seventeen years earlier (see Chapter 10), had proved to be a lesson well learned. Applications were refused for a Hoop-la stall and for 'an entertainment known as Housey-Housey.' And in 1929 the Sands and Entertainments Committee recommended that speedboats should not be allowed.

Information about the resort in the 1930's is to be found in the official holiday guides. It is evident that Redcar then had many more amenities to offer its visitors. The sandbanks had been transformed into the Stray, now recognised as a priceless asset to the town. The Stray then boasted a miniature golf course (closed 1978) and a children's paddling pool (reduced and remodelled 1979). The Promenade, stretching for three miles, was at its most attractive. The central portion between the bandstand and the pier was set out with flower beds and during August fairylights illuminated the Promenade, the Bandstand and New Pavilion. Three parks had been created, each with its own tennis courts, bowling greens and other recreational facilities.

THE COATHAM ENCLOSURE

Ambitious schemes had been carried out near the Coatham Convalescent Home, in what was to be the Coatham Enclosure. A boating lake, two open air pools and an indoor swimming bath had been built. The surrounding area had been attractively laid out with lawns, flower beds, fountains and paths. During August, myriads of fairylights transformed the area into a 'land of enchantment.' A Children's Day Nursery was established in what is now the boathouse. Mothers could leave their children for a few hours knowing that while they enjoyed a peaceful stroll along the Promenade, the youngsters would be well cared for. The Nursery was opened in 1925 by the Marchioness of Zetland and it was organised and run by the Mayoress, Mrs. B. O. Davies and a committee of townspeople, supported by voluntary donations.

South of the railway, along West Dyke Road, was the **Pleasure Park**. Opened in 1925, it entertained visitors and residents alike until the land was sold in 1938. In 1937 its attractions included the Noah's Ark, Hilarity Hall and Scenic Motors. The Giant Racer was claimed to be the largest and most up to date in the provinces; there was a fine panoramic view from the Tees round to Huntcliff when the cars reached the top, before their nerve-shattering plunge down the swooping track. The latest addition to the Pleasure Park was a skating rink, said to be the largest covered skating rink in the north.

Film lovers were well catered for. In 1937 there were three cinemas in the town. There was the Palace on the Esplanade, the Central Cinema opened in the old Central Hall, once the railway station; adjoining it was the Regent Cinema. The Palace closed as a cinema in the 1960's and offered prize-bingo instead. It was a loss on two counts; it had always prided itself in being in the fore-front of cinema development — it was one of the first in the north-east to show talking pictures, and it was the only cinema in town with double seats at the rear of the stalls—much loved by courting couples of the day! The Central was almost totally destroyed by fire in 1948 but reopened in the 1950's. The Regent was also used once or twice by the local operatic society for pantomimes. Both the Central and the Regent were lost when the building was demolished in 1964 and the new shops and offices of Craigton House built in their place. The name of the Regent lives on in what was the New Pavilion. The Palace closed in 1979 and the property was sold.

Concert parties were held in the New Pavilion, erected in 1928 over the roof of the long defunct Coatham Pier. The New Pavilion was entirely glass roofed and was reputedly the warmest and cosiest hall in town. It is still known affectionately by some older residents as the 'glasshouse.' It seated 800 in 'the latest plush chairs of very comfortable design.'

Dances were held at the Pier Pavilion and at hotels throughout the town. Billy Scarrow's 'Optimists' appeared on the pierrot pitch on the beach. For the children there was of course Punch and Judy and a ventriloquist and, in 1937, a special children's corner was created.

THE CORONATION OF KING GEORGE VI

For the first time, the entire Coronation Service was broadcast on the radio from Westminster Abbey. Throughout the service, the streets of Redcar were deserted, almost the entire population was at home listening to the broadcast.

The poor weather was not allowed to spoil the events planned to celebrate the great day. The dull sky was countered by the gaily decorated streets. Union flags stretched taut in the stiff breeze. Hanging crowns swung to and fro amid garlands of red white and blue. A prize was won by Hintons, in the High Street, for the best decorated business premises. Charles Street won the prize for the best decorated street in town. There were also prizes for the best decorated houses in each ward and even for the best decorated boats on the sea front. The local celebrations all went without a hitch. The Mayor toured the schools and each child was given a copy of the souvenir programme and a quarter pound tin of Rowntrees chocolates. It was estimated at the time, that nearly half the children in the town attended the many parties held in the streets. Towards the end of the week, the Corporation acted as hosts to the children of the Borough and took them to cinemas to see newsreels of the Coronation.

The old people of the town were to be taken on a rail excursion to Whitby. Heavy rain dampened their spirits as the party assembled at Redcar Central Station. It was too late to postpone or re-arrange the outing so at the last minute, Mr. Billy Scarrow was asked to take his Pierrots to Whitby. This he did and the old folk enjoyed an afternoon of entertainment at the Spa Hall which was placed at their disposal by Whitby Urban Council. On the return rail journey, afternoon tea was served.

In the evening crowds thronged the streets, in readiness for the torchlight procession and firework display. About 9 p.m. the procession left Ridley House on Coatham Road and, followed by hundreds of spectators, marched through the town to the Stray where the Mayor lit a bonfire. A firewoks display followed, crowned by set pieces of portraits of the King and Queen which were greeted with prolonged clapping and cheering. After the fireworks there was dancing on the Stray. Dormanstown and Warrenby had their own bonfires and fireworks displays.

Later, the Mayor, Councillor Nixon, reported that he had received 160 pairs of boots from the Middlesbrough Co-operative Society Ltd., at a Coronation Gift for distribution to needy families in the Borough.

CHAPTER FIFTEEN — 1939 - 1945
WORLD WAR II 1939–45

THE Redcar season came to an abrupt end on 3rd September, 1939, when Great Britain declared war on Germany. Preparations had been made since the beginning of the year, in readiness for the emergency. A local National Service Committee was appointed for Redcar in January 1939 and a few months later, a National Service Rally was held in the New Pavilion. Volunteers were also needed to complete Redcar's Civil Defence Services — to fill such posts are air raid wardens, first aid parties, special constables, ambulance drivers and auxiliary firemen.

In March, the A.R.P. committee was given permission to use the site of the Isolation Hospital at Grewgrass Farm for the volunteers' outdoor training. At the same time, the Local Defence Volunteers were drilling in the Territorial Army Hall, which then stood in the High Street, opposite the Swan Hotel. In June, the respirators allocated to the town were ready for distribution; children received theirs through the schools. An attack using chemical gas which would incapacitate or kill large numbers of the population was considered a serious threat so gas masks were distributed throughout the country. There were adults masks, children's masks and even an all-enveloping bag with a window and respirator to protect small babies.

Redcar had been included in a list of areas ' exposed to the liability of air attack.' All families who were able to do so, were expected to arrange for their own protection. Those families with large enough gardens built Anderson shelters; a pit in the ground was covered with curved corrugated metal sheets, forming an arched roof which in turn was covered with the earth dug from the pit. This was expected to provide protection from flying debris but would not withstand a direct hit. Many homes without gardens installed Morrison shelters; these resembled a very sturdy steel table, the sides between the legs were filled with a stout steel mesh with an entrance at one end. In the event of a bombing raid, the family sheltered under the steel table which was expected to protect them if the house collapsed around them. There were public shelters in Wilton Street and certain other side streets and the cellars of some public houses were used as shelters by neighbouring families.

The North Riding County Council was responsible for the

provision of public shelters in Redcar. In September 1939 they bought twenty cast-iron shelters, each designed to shelter fifty people. These metal shelters were later replaced when it was realised that they would shatter on impact and were potentially dangerous. To protect shoppers, shelters were erected in the High Street ; one stood near the Town Clock, with a static water tank beside it. There were several others further along the High Street, where the road widens.

There were air raid wardens posts in each ward of the Borough. At first the headquarters of the Rescue services was in the concrete shelters under the Bandstand. After a high tide flooded the room a new Report Centre was set up in the boathouse in Locke Park.

REDCAR AT WAR

In 1940 fear of invasion was rife. Direction and other road signs were removed and road barriers set up throughout the area, including barriers across Granville Terrace and Corporation Road.

The military authorities closed the pier in September 1940 and two sections were removed to hinder the enemy in the event of invasion. The sand dunes adjacent to the golf course were sewn with land mines. Barbed wire stretched from South Gare to Marske. On the Promenade masses of barbed wire were twisted round the railings, giving the resort a very grim countenance.

The side streets leading to the High Street from the Promenade were barricaded with huge blocks of concrete, leaving gaps wide enough to admit only one person at a time. Similar blocks were set on the slipways, restricting access to the beach. The beach itself was littered with concrete blocks linked with steel wires, and set in the sands were steel spikes designed to hinder the movement of enemy tanks. The beach was of course closed to the public during the early years of the war. Fishermen and residents gathering sea-coal were issued with special permits allowing them on the sands, by the police. They were only allowed on the stretch of beach between Redcar Pier and the Coatham Enclosure. No one was allowed on the Stray where the coastal defences consisted of concrete pill-boxes, machine guns and searchlights. Between Marske and Redcar, the Stray was sewn with land mines. There were ack-ack guns in the rugby field near Green Lane.

At the beginning of 1940, over three hundred soldiers were billeted on the racecourse, as an overflow from the camp at Marske. Troops were also stationed at Coatham Convalescent Home and at Kirkleatham Hall. Some servicemen were billeted in private homes in the town.

The RAF took over the New Pavilion in June 1941. A month later they closed Granville Terrace and the Promenade, using the roads for training purposes. Later they transferred their drill exercises to the car park at Fishermen's Square.

AIR RAIDS IN REDCAR

The first evidence of air raid damage to the town appears in the Council Mnutes in June 1941. There was 'substantial damage sustained by part of the town as a result of enemy action in May.' Approximately 2,000 windows were blown out and between 200 and 300 roofs damaged.

Undoubtedly the air raid which caused most damage to life, property and morale occurred on 21st October, 1941. Three high explosive bombs fell on East Coatham Ward. The first struck Dr. Robinson's house, killing his housekeeper. The second was a direct hit on the Zetland Club, killing the Mayor of Redcar, Alderman Charlie Harris, Councillor J. Roebuck, Dr. Robinson and several other prominent citizens. The third bomb damaged number 46 Queen Street but caused no deaths. A memorial service was held in St. Peter's Church for the fifteen people killed in this raid. About ten years after the war, in the mid-fifties, the site of the Zetland Club, opposite the Cenotaph in Coatham Road, was turned into an ornamental garden.

Warrenby Works suffered several air raids. On Saturday, 15th November, 1941, a low flying German plane dropped two high explosive bombs damaging a blast furnace. This raid nearly beat the air raid warning system and the sirens were still sounding as the bombs fell. Casualties were high; ten men were killed and forty-nine men and women injured. The Medical Officer's report for the last quarter of 1941 shows that half the deaths in the town were 'due to war operations.'

Two months after the last raid, on Tuesday, 13th January, 1942, four H.E. bombs fell on Warrenby Steel Works; again, ten men were killed and about thirty men and women injured.

Most of the serious raids on the district were concentrated in that period from October 1941 to the Spring of 1942. The chilling howls of the air raid sirens, as the notes rose and fell to give warning of a coming raid, followed later by the long steady note of the 'all clear' were a regular feature of war time life.

A blast wall was constructed round the front of the old lifeboat house in April 1942, to protect the old lifeboat 'Zetland.' Some private houses had blast walls built in front of groundfloor windows; one remained in Gordon Road until 1958. Other private houses had brick-built air raid shelters in the gardens. One in Kirkleatham Lane had internal dimensions about four feet by six feet by eight feet high; the walls were built of three courses of bricks, 16 inches thick and a steel rod reinforced roof. It was demolished in 1959 and some of the rubble was buried in the garden, rather than cart it away!

Dormanstown did not escape the air raids unscathed. An unexploded bomb in Wilton Avenue led to the evacuation of more than one hundred people in December 1942. The Emergency Meals Service provided mid-day meals for the evacuees at the Dormanstown Rest Centre.

The last serious bombing of the district was on 22nd March, 1943. There were no casualties but three houses at the east end of the town were severely damaged and several others to a lesser extent. One unexploded 'fire pot' hit number 1 Cypress Road and another hit 25 and 27 Zetland Road. Number 13 Chestnut Avenue was hit by an unexploded shell.*

Thirty-seven people were killed in air raids in the Borough of Redcar during the war. The figure might well have been higher because the nearby iron and steelworks were important targets to the Germans. Mercifully many bombs missed their targets and fell in the sea, in the marshes near Warrenby and in the open country between the town and the Cleveland Hills.

RE-OPENING THE BEACH

The Corporation asked, in June 1941, for a restricted portion of the beach — between the pier and the New Pavilion — to be made available to the public. The military authorities refused in case it led to an influx of visitors to the town. The following

---

*This account of air raids on Redcar is based on the Air Raid Wardens reports, in the Cleveland County Archives.

year, a fresh application was made to the military authorities at Marske and Kirkleatham, and also to the Superintendent of Police at Redcar. To no avail, the beach remained closed for another year.

In the Summer of 1943, the Corporation received a letter from the Military Commander stating that he would allow the re-opening of Redcar beach within certain limits and subject to the following conditions :

(i) The only permitted access to the beach was to be via the slipway opposite Moore Street.
(ii) The beach would be open only until 30th September, 1943. Hours of opening were 10 a.m. to 12-30 p.m. and 2 p.m. to 5 p.m. The beach could be closed at any time at the discretion of the Commander.
(iii) The Corporation were to provide wardens responsible for the control of the public within the specified boundaries. Sea bathing and boat trips were prohibited. Dogs and unaccompanied children were not permitted on the beach.

Despite the restrictions, the beach was so popular that an extension was sought and the beach remained open until the end of October. The beach was again opened in the Summer of 1944, subject to the same conditions with a few amendments. The public was warned of a tarred trench across the sands.

PEACE IN SIGHT

By the Autumn of 1944, it appeared that the danger was passed and the end of the war might be in sight. In October, the military road barriers were removed. In November work started on clearing the minefields. The Invasion Committee was disbanded and reductions were made in the Civil Defence and Fire Guard Services.

In 1945, the Regional Commissioner opened the whole of the beaches within the Borough, excepting only the stretch of sand from Coatham Promenade to the South Gare breakwater ; in this area a number of mines were not accounted for.

In April 1945, the Corporation began to plan the celebrations that would mark the end of hostilities in Europe. There was to be a civic service in the forecourt of the Municipal Buildings on the day following the announcement of the end of the war. The

Municipal Buildings were to be decorated with flags and to be floodlit in the evening. The New Pavilion and the Bandstand would also be illuminated and a band was to play on the Promenade again.

V.E. DAY CELEBRATIONS

All German forces unconditionally surrendered to the Western Allies on Tuesday, 8th May, 1945, and Victory in Europe was declared. Within 48 hours England was a blaze of colour and rejoicing. Redcar was bedecked with flags, streamers fluttered from windows and streets were criss-crossed with bunting. Many streets organised ' Victory Teas ' for children ; one of the largest was in Whitby Crescent where, as well as a tea, the children had roundabouts and a Punch and Judy show.

Marina Avenue also had a large tea party. The huge cake, in the centre of a table laden with food — remember food was still rationed — was cut by the Vicar of Coatham. After tea, the children were given ice-cream and donkey rides. Hanging in the middle of the street was an effigy of Adolf Hitler which was shot later in the day. There were sports during the evening and a piano was carried out into the street for dancing and musical games. To complete the evening, everyone went to the beach and sang round a bonfire.

A great number of townspeople turned out for Redcar's Thanksgiving Day Parade, despite the heavy rain. Many local organisations were represented in the procession which the Mayor led from the Municipal Buildings to the Regent and Central Cinemas where the services where held. On returning to the Municipal Buildings, the Mayor laid a wreath at the War Memorial ' From the Citizens of Redcar.'

AFTERMATH

Redcar survived the Second World War and for a while in the 1950's was restored to its former popularity as a resort. Trends changed, fewer people stayed for a week, let alone a month as they had done in Victorian times. The era of the day-tripper arrived. A flood of several thousand 'trippers' was a common sight as the excursion trains set down their passengers at the Special Platform in Kirkleatham Street and the mass of people moved down Station Road to the sea front. On race days it was quite commonplace to see convoys of sixteen or eighteen coaches driving down from Durham as virtually entire communities came for a day at Redcar — the men to the races, the wives and children on the beach. These golden days were short lived as personal prosperity grew after the war and people took to 'package' holidays in Mediterranean resorts. Redcar became, as it is now, a dormitory for the industrial workers of Tees-side. The sea front remains colourful with fishing boats drawn up along the sea wall and a range of roundabouts, swings and amusement arcades for visitors. The gardens and illuminations are gone from the promenade, tennis courts have been removed from Zetland Park and the miniature golf has gone from the stray.

POLITICAL CHANGE

Redcar Borough Council was amalgamated with Middlesbrough County Council, Stockton Borough Council and the Urban Districts of Eston and Billingham, forming the County Borough of Teesside in 1968. In 1974 the local government boundaries were completely re-organised throughout the country. Redcar, although still recognisable as a separate town became part of Langbaurgh Borough Council, in the new county of Cleveland.

In the Spring of 1984 the Municipal Buildings on Coatham Road were demolished. They had been used by Redcar Borough Council, Teesside County Council and Langbaurgh Borough Council successively. A block of flats has been built on the site, only the Cenotaph remains.

PRINCIPAL EVENTS IN REDCAR

June 1855—Board of Health formed for Redcar.

April 1876—Extension of Parish of Redcar by inclusion of portion of Marske and Upleatham.

Sept. 1877—Board of Health formed for Kirkleatham, including Coatham.

Dec. 1894—First Elections of Redcar and Kirkleatham Urban Councils.

April 1895—Membership of Redcar Urban District Council increased.

April 1899—Amalgamation of Redcar and Coatham in one Urban District.

April 1910—Urban District divided into four Wards.

Jan. 1916—Foundation of Village of Dormanstown.

Sept. 1920—Purchase of the Gas Works by Urban District Council.

Oct. 1920—Extension of Urban District of Redcar to Lazenby Station.

Dec. 1920—Movement for Incorporation launched.

June 1921—Inquiry by the Privy Council.

July 1921—Provisional grant of a Charter.

Sept. 1921—Burial Board area extended to whole Urban District.

April 1922—Urban District divided into six Wards.

May 1922—His Majesty the King grants Redcar its Charter.

Nov. 1922—First Meeting of the Mayor, Aldermen and Councillors of the Borough of Redcar.

Nov. 1922—Opening of the New Trunk Road from Redcar to Grangetown.

June 1923—New Shelters opened.

Nov. 1923—New Coast Road to Marske officially opened.

Nov. 1923—Start made with the new cottages for the working classes.

Dec. 1923—Gas supply extended to Dormanstown.

Dec. 1923—Order for supply of electricity granted by Electricity Commissioners.

Dec. 1923—Gift of land for Zetland Park by the Marquess of Zetland.

Feb. 1924—Purchase of foreshore rights completed.

June 1924—Opening of Borough and Zetland Parks.

Sept. 1924—Installation of Electric Lighting.

Oct. 1924—New gas holder completed.

Nov. 1924—Water Carriage System completed.

Dec. 1924—Gift of Locke Park to the Borough.

July 1925—Day Nursery started.

Aug. 1925—New Infectious Diseases Hospital opened.

Aug. 1925—Completion of Coatham Promenade extension and enclosure.

Nov. 1925—Dormanstown Housing Scheme completed.

Dec. 1925—Redcar Housing Schemes finished.

Sept. 1926—Freedom of Borough conferred upon Mr. A. O. Cochrane, J.P. (First Freeman).

Oct. 1926—Norton House purchased.

Nov. 1926—War Memorial unveiled.

Oct. 1927—Adoption of Coke Oven Gas.

June 1928—Municipal Pavilion opened.

July 1928—Centenary of Lifeboat Station.

Oct. 1928—Gift of six acres of land as Children's Playing Fields.

June 1929—Opening of Locke Park Lake.

July 1929—Opening of Beach Walk and Western Promenade.

Sept. 1929—Opening of Newcomen Playing Field.

Oct. 1929—Opening of Dormanstown Playing Field.

Oct. 1929—Crescent Housing Estate completed.

May 1930—Locke Park completed.

June 1930—Coatham Boating Lake opened.

July 1930—Open Air Pool formally opened.

Nov. 1930—Covered Baths completed.

June 1931—Homes for Aged Persons opened.

June 1931—Construction of Wiley Brigg Road completed.

Oct. 1931—Second Dormanstown Housing Programme finished.

Dec. 1931—Opening of new Subway on Crescent Estate.

April 1932—Extension of Borough by 900 acres.

May 1932—Ridley House bought by Council.

Sept. 1932—Freedom of the Borough conferred upon Alderman Davies, J.P., C.C.

Dec. 1932—Aged Homes opened at Warrenby.

June 1933—Purchase of additional foreshore.

July 1933—Second Instalment of Aged Homes completed at Redcar.

Aug. 1933—Purchase of Old Market Hall, High Street, Redcar.

Nov. 1934—Opening of Robert McClean Memorial Homes for Aged Persons.

Oct. 1935—Plaque erected on Red Barns to the memory of Miss Gertrude L. Bell.

Oct. 1935—Adoption of Libraries Acts.

Nov. 1935—Reconstruction of Reservoir at Upleatham commenced.

Jan. 1936—Adoption of Small Dwellings Acquisition Act 1899–1935.

July 1936—Opening of " Robert McClean " Memorial Homes.

Nov. 1936—Reconstruction of the Reservoir completed.

April 1937—Permanent Fire Brigade formed.

July 1937—New Gas Showrooms in High Street opened.

Sept. 1937—New Electricity Shoowrooms, offices and premises of Electricity Department opened.

Dec. 1937—Opening of Public Library at Ridley House, by Archbishop of York.

Dec. 1937—Purchase of additional Foreshore, etc.

July 1938—Redcar Corporation Act, 1938, received Royal Assent.

July 1941—Freedom of the Borough conferred on Alderman W. Wardman, J.P., C.C.

May 1947—Silver Jubilee of Charter of Incorporation.

May 1947—Freedom of the Borough conferred on Alderman Mrs. I. Lonsdale, M.B.E., C.C.

April 1948—Fire Brigade transferred to North Riding County Council.

July 1948 –Electricity Undertaking transferred to North Eastern Electricity Board.

May 1949—Gas Undertaking transferred to Northern Gas Board.

May 1951—Adaptation of Open Air Swimming Pool as a Roller Skating Rink completed.

May 1951—Freedom of the Borough conferred on Mr. A. W. Chaplin and Alderman J. Coupland, J.P., C.C.

June 1951—Visit of H.M.S. Agincourt—Festival of Britain Celebrations.

Aug. 1951—Visit of H.R.H. Princess Royal on the occasion of the naming of the new Redcar Lifeboat " City of Leeds."

May 1953—Visit of H.M.S. Battleaxe—Coronation Celebrations.

June 1953—Celebration of the Coronation of Her Majesty Queen Elizabeth II.

May 1956—Visit of Her Majesty Queen Elizabeth II to I.C.I. Ltd., Wilton Works.

April 1958—Water Undertaking transferred to Tees Valley and Cleveland Water Board.

Dec. 1958—Freedom of Entry into the Borough conferred upon the Green Howards Regiment.

Feb. 1960—Dormanstown Branch Library opened.

Jan. 1961—Freedom of the Borough conferred upon Ald. R. J. Gillingham.

Jan. 1963—Revision of Ward Boundaries.

June 1963—Coatham Bay Caravan Site opened.

Feb. 1964—Roseberry Square Shopping Centre opened.

Nov. 1965—Laburnum Road Branch Library opened.

Feb. 1967—Roseberry Branch Library opened.

CHAIRMEN OF REDCAR URBAN DISTRICT COUNCIL SINCE AMALGAMATION OF AREAS

1899–1900	James Crosby Robson.
1900–1901	John Bulmer.
1901–1902	James Crosby Robson.
1902–1903	Thomas Phillipson.
1903–1904	Henry Walker.
1904–1905	John Bulmer and Thomas Phillipson.
1905–1906	Henry Hudson.
1906–1907	William Baker.
1907–1908	John William Storrow.
1908–1909	William Wardman.
1909–1910	Walter Sacker Hill.
1910–1911	John Scott.
1911–1912	Henry Hudson.
1912–1913	Thomas Wrightson.
1913–1914	John Hutton.
1914–1915	Joseph Tomlinson.
1915–1916	William Metcalf.
1916–1917	Thomas Phillipson.
1917–1918	Thomas Phillipson.
1918–1919	Arthur Malthouse Hall.
1919–1920	James Smart Crone.
1920–1921	James Smart Crone and William Wardman.
1921–1922	Benjamin Owen Davies.

LIST OF MAYORS

1922	Benjamin Owen Davies (Ship-owner).
1923	Benjamin Owen Davies (Ship-owner).
1924	Benjamin Owen Davies (Ship-owner).
1925	William Wardman (Retired Architect).
1926	Walter Sacker Hill (Retired Works Manager).
1927	Walter Sacker Hill (Retired Works Manager).
1928	William Metcalf (Retired Draper).
1929	William Metcalf (Retired Draper).
1930	John Emmerson Batty (Retired China Merchant).
1931	Isabel Lonsdale (Cafe Proprietress).
1932	William Charlton (Retired Confectioner).
1933	William Morris (Works Director).
1934	William Morris (Works Director).
1935	John William Farren (Insurance District Manager).
1936	John Robert Nixon (Insurance Official).
1937	David Roddie Semple (Mill Manager).
1938	Richard Spellman (Coal Merchant).
1939	Joseph Coupland (Blast Furnaceman).
1940	Charlie Harris (Dock Officer).
1941	Wm. Arthur Place (Storekeeper).
1942	Geo. Cruddas (Company Director).
1943	Albert Walker Chaplin (Hotel Proprietor).
1944	James Thomas Fletcher (Master Plumber).
1945	John Spurr Dixon (Tees Pilot).
1946	Robert James Gillingham (Painter).
1947	Sydney George Shillito (Retired Detective Inspector).
1949	Fred Laidley Wilson (Gentleman).
1950	James William Coles (General Secretary).
1951	Thomas Alexander Dougall (Master Baker).
1952	Robert Hodgart Cowie (Company Director).
1953	William Atkinson (Partner in Pork Butchering Business).
1954	Reginald Kistler (Area Sales Executive).
1954	George Fall Andrew (Head Timekeeper).
1955	Edward Bradburn (Company Director).
1956	Charles Rand (Retired Assurance Superintendent).
1957	Stanley Linford (Engineer).
1958	Ronald Hall (Master Decorator).
1959	Henry Armstrong Darling (Retired Shopkeeper).
1960	George William Thorne (Fitter and Turner).
1961	Philip Harvey (School Teacher).
1962	Albert William Kidd (Steelworks Staff Employee).
1963	Stanley Brotton (Crane Driver).
1964	Joseph Coupland (Retired Blastfurnaceman).
1965	Gordon Timperley Thornton (Town Planning Consultant).
1966	Lancelot Harold Barker (Farmer).
1967	**Hannah Cunningham (Housewife).**
1968	**Redcar became part of Teesside County Borough.**

Bibliography

The History of Cleveland, 1808, John Graves

A Trip to Coatham, 1810, W. Hutton

The Visitors' Guide to Redcar, 1841, John Walbran

The History and Antiquities of Cleveland, 1846, John Walker Ord

The Visitors' Guide to Redcar, 1848, John Walbran

Visitors' Handbook to Redcar, Coatham and Saltburn-by-Sea, 1863, Tweddell

Rambles Through Redcar, Saltburn and Neighbourhood, 1888, Angus Macpherson

History of Cleveland, Ancient and Modern, Vol. 2, J. C. Atkinson

The Local Records of Stockton and the Neighbourhood, Thomas Richmond

A Short History of Redcar Racecourse, J. Fairfax Blakeborough

Railways in Cleveland, K. Hoole

North Eastern Railway, Wm. Weaver Tomlinson

Shipwrecks of the Yorkshire Coast, A. Godfrey & P. J. Lassey

Redcar in Retrospect, Peter Sotheran

The History of Marske-by-Sea, Edmund Hope

History of Local Government in Redcar, 1855-1923, R. McClean

Everyday Hero — The Story of a Yorkshire Fisherman, D. Phillipson

Building in the British Economy between the Wars, H. W. Richardson & D. H. Aldcroft

Directories and Gazetteers

Langdale, Thomas, *A. Topographical Dictionary of Yorkshire*, 2nd ed., 1822

Baines, Edward, *History Directory and Gazetteer of the County of Yorkshire*, Vol. 2, 1823

White, William, *History, Gazetteer and Directory of the East and North Ridings of Yorkshire*, 1840

Slater's, *Royal National Commercial Directory of the Counties of Cumberland, Durham, Northumberland, Westmorland and the Cleveland District*, 1876-1877

Bulmer, T., *History, Topography and Directory of North Yorkshire*, 1890

Kelly's Directories for North & East Ridings of Yorkshire, 1909, 1913, 1925, 1929

Redcar for Happy Holidays, 1933, Redcar Borough Council

Redcar for Health, 1937, Redcar Borough Council

A Pictorial & Descriptive Guide to Whitby & District including Redcar, 7th edn., revised, Ward Lock

Old Newspapers

Yorkshire Gazette
Middlesbrough News and Cleveland Advertiser
Daily Exchange
Weekly Exchange
Redcar and Saltburn News, 1900-1916
Redcar and Saltburn Gazette
The Cleveland Standard, 1922-1945
Evening Gazette, 1922, 1924-25, 1929-30, 1937

Maps and Plans

Ordnance Survey Maps, 1851 and 1895
Plan of Redcar, 1815 (from Zetland Collection)
Peat's Plan of Redcar, 1861

Census Returns

Redcar, 1851 and 1871
Coatham, 1851 and 1871

Council Records

Redcar Local Board of Health Minutes, 1860-1894
Kirkleatham Local Board of Health Minutes, 1877-1894
Redcar Urban District Council Minutes, 1894-1899 & 1900-1922
Kirkleatham Urban District Council Minutes, 1894-1899
Redcar (and Coatham) Urban District Council Minutes, 1899-1901
Redcar Borough Council Minutes, 1922-1945

School Records
Zetland School Log Books, 1863-1901

Sanitary Reports
Superintending Inspector's Report to the General Board of Health on the Sanitary Condition of Redcar, 1855

A Special Report on the Sanitary Condition of Redcar

A Special Report on the Sanitary Conditions of Kirkleatham District with Reference to the State of Preparedness to Withstand any Invasion of Cholera

Report by Dr. Barry on Enteric Fever in Tees Valley Towns

Miscellaneous
Prospects of the Redcar Railway

Proposed Asylum Harbour and Naval Station at Redcar on the Coast of Yorkshire . . . to be Called Port William, 1834, W. A. Brookes

Redcar and Coatham Literary Institute Exhibition News, 1901, 1901-2, 1903

Memorial . . . of an Indenture Bearing the date 10th May, 1862, Between Teresa Newcomen and Rev. John Postlethwaite . . . Concerning Coatham Common

Declaration of Trust in Respect of the Coatham Convalescent Home and Children's Hospital, dated 25th April, 1893, Mary Postlethwaite and others

The Cleveland and Teesside Local History Session Bulletin II, December 1970

The Port of Coatham, 1789 to 1808, D. W. Pattenden

A Parting Word, or Redcar as it is and Redcar as it should be, Unknown Writer, 1864

Air Raid Wardens' Reports, World War II, Cleveland County Archives

Official Opening of Redcar Library, Teesside County Borough Council

INDEX

	Page
Abercrombie Road	115
Academy, The	27
Adshead Road	115
Aeroplanes, various	100
Aeroplanes, complaints about	101
Agar, John Yeoman	25
Air Raids	132
Air Station, Royal Naval	100
Albert Street	73, 119
Albion Terrace	40, 48
Alexandra Hotel (Pig & Whistle)	120
Alfred Street	86
All Saints Church, Dormanstown	123
Alma Parade	73
Amalgamation of Redcar and Coatham	81
Amarant, Wreck of	80
Anderson Shelters	130
Angles, The	9
A.R.P. Committee	130
Arthur Place (Railway Terrace)	119
Back Lane	40, 43
Back to Back Housing	44
Baine's Directory of Yorkshire	27
Bandstand	91, 92, 126
Bank Street (German Street)	119
Bathing	
At Coatham	18
At Redcar	18, 27, 48
Regulations	93, 126
Bathing Machines	126
Baths	20
Beach	
Amusements on	93, 94, 126
Foreshore, Rights of	121
Forest on	11
Re-opening after War	133
War-time Defences, Clearance	99, 131
Bean's Field	100
Beech Avenue	115
Bell, Gertrude L and Thomas Hugh	57
Bellasis, Richard, Brian Charles	13, 14
Bentinck Terrace (Coatham Road)	56, 119
Beresford-Pierse, Sir Henry	109
Billy Scarrow's Pierrots	70, 128
Birdsall Row	73

	Page
Birger, Wreck of	70, 80
Billeting of Soldiers	132
Blast Furnacemen, Working Hours of	60
Blatherwick, Ann	24
Boating Lake	112, 127
Boer War	83
Boiler Explosion at Warrenby	79
Bombardment of Hartlepool	97
Bombing Targets	100
Broadway East	115, 119
Borough of Redcar	
Gifts to	107
Incorporation Day	106
Borough Park	110
Boulby Road	117
Boundary Fence	63
British Legion	103
Brookes, Mr. A. W.	30
Brooksbank Avenue	113
Brothers, St. John Dancers	96
Brothers, The (Lifeboat)	80
Brus de, Lucy and Robert	14
Buckingham Road	117
Bulmer, John	88
Cambridge Terrace (Redcar Lane)	119
Canterbury Road	117
Carnegie Trust, Library	125
Caroline, Wreck of	31
Carter's Baths	20
Cedar Grove	116
Census Figures	16, 32, 38, 55, 57, 83
Central Cinema	70, 95, 127, 128
Central Hall	70, 90, 95, 127
Chaloner, Admiral	68
Changes in Street Names	41, 118
Charles Street	86
Charlotte Street	86
Cheshire Home, Marske	29
Chester Road	117
Cholera, Preparations to withstand	74
Cholera Outbreak	42
Christ Church, Coatham	52, 103
Church Street (Redcar Lane)	41, 119
Churches — see under dedication or Redcar, Coatham, etc.	
Cinemas	70, 95, 127
Fire at Central Cinema	128
Civil Parishes, Union of	104
Clarendon Terrace	40, 48

146

Clarendon Street	55
Cleveland and Durham Electricity Supply Company	89
Cleveland Terrace (Coatham Road)	73, 119
Cleveland Water Co.	79
Cleveland Place (Railway Terrace)	119
Cleveland Standard	
Report of 1916	99
Report of 1920	104, 113
Cliff House, Marske	28
Coast Road, Construction of	110
Coastal Guard Works, Suveyor of	100
Coatham	
Bathing	18
Boating Lake	112, 127
Changes of Road Names	41
Church	103
Church Hall	11
Convalescent Home	53, 98
C. of E. School	52
Declining Popularity	27
Free School	27
Grammar School	53
Ings, East and West	13
Iron Works	59
Pier	69, 81, 95
Population	16, 32, 38, 57, 63, 83
Port	25
Road	56
Water Supply	33
Windmill	41
Yeoman's House	24
Coat of Arms, Redcar	5
Cochrane, S.S., Wreck of	69
Commission of Inquiry, 1575	12
Coney Street	61
Convalescent Home	53, 98
Conway Road	119
Cook, Captain James	20
Coronations	84, 90, 128
Corporation Road, Construction of	109
Corrymbus, Wreck of	69
Cosy Corner	70
Coulthirst, Robert	13
Craigton House, Queen Street	128
Crescent, The	117
Cricket Club	117
Crown and Anchor	24
Cruck Houses	22
Cypress Road	117

	Page
Daisy Road (Windsor Road)	119
Danes, The	10, 13
Davies, Councillor and Mrs. B. O.	106, 111, 121
Davies, B. O., Health Centre	125
Day Nursery	127
Defence Volunteers	130
Dickens, Charles	50
Directory of 1840, White's	32
Domesday Book	10
Dorman, Long & Co.	104, 112, 116, 123
Dorman Memorial Home	117
Dorman, Clara Lady and Mr. Charles	102, 122
Dormanstown	118
Church	122
Garden City	104
Population	120
School	122
Union with Redcar	105
Downey & Co.	59
Downey Street	61
Dr. Horner's Hydropathic Establishment	48
Duck Trapping, Coatham Marshes	33
Dundas Place (High Street)	41, 48
Dundas Street	55
Durham Miners Strike	61
Easson Road	87
East Halt Station	112
Education Committee	124
Electricity Supply	89, 121
Elm Road	115
Elton Street	73
Ely Crescent	117
Enteric Fever, Report of 1893 on	77
Esk, Wreck of	29
Esplanade	40, 44, 48, 49
Ex-Servicemen's Association	102
Fairbridge Place	73
Fallow, Thomas MaCall	11
Fauconberg, Lord Walter de	11
Fever Hospital	11
Fire Stations	65, 66, 88
Fishermen's Square	40, 42
Fishing	33
Fleck, Family of Captain James Cook	20
Foreshore Rights	121
Forest on Beach	11
France Street	119

	Page
Garden City (Dormanstown)	104
Gas Company, Redcar	45, 104
Gaunt Family and Salmon Fishing	33
General Purposes Committee	126
George Street	87
George Terrace (Redcar Lane)	119
German Street (Bank Street)	119
Gertrude, Wreck of	84
Glass House	70, 128
Globe Hotel	55
Graffenburg Street	55
Grant Street	73
Granville Terrace	48
Grave's History of Cleveland	17
Green Lane Military Camp	98
Grew Grass Farm	122, 130
Griffin, Wreck of	69
Grove's Pierrots	85
Guardians of Poor	43
Guisborough	
Work House	20
Poor Law Union	42
Rural District Council	105
Sanitary Authority	63
Guy's Yard	55
Hall, Mrs. Mary	24
Hanson Street	86
Harbour Schemes	30
Hardy, Private	83
Harris, Alderman Charlie, Mayor	132
Harrison, Mr. John	124
Hawthorne, Nathaniel	50
Health Standards, Ranger Report on	43
Hearse Street (Stanley Grove)	119
Henry Street	73
High Street, Coatham	119
High Street, Redcar	24, 40, 41, 48, 55, 119
Hintons	128
History of Cleveland by Graves	17
Hobson's Terrace (West Dyke Road)	41
Hodgson Terrace	86
Holder Street	86
Honoraria, Wreck of	84
Housing	
Council Development	113
Council Rents	116
Development Peak	116
Homeless People	113

	Page
Private Development	116
Rents for Old People's Homes	118
Temporary	113
Huntcliffe View	114
Hutton's Trip to Coatham	17
Hydropathic Establishment, Dr. Horner's	48
Illuminations	121, 126
Incorporation of Redcar Borough Council	106
Inquiry, Commission of 1575	12
Iron Works, Coatham	59
Ironstone Mining	
Decline of	73
Its Effect on Area	58
Upleatham	36
Ironworks Band, Redcar	98
Ironworks, Redcar	104
Isolation Hospital, Grewgrass Farm	76, 122, 130
Jolly Sailor Inn	27
Kettleness Avenue	117
King Edward VII	
Coronation of	84
Memorial Clock	85
King George V, Coronation of	90
King George VI, Coronation of	128
King James Terrace	41
King Street	55
Kirkleatham Street	73
Kirkleatham	
Hall	99
Estates	16, 109, 115, 121
Church	13
Local Health Board	63, 64, 79, 105
Manor	14
Parish	16
Population	16, 32
School Board	52
Water Supply	77
Laburnum Road	116, 118
Langbaurgh Borough Council	56, 136
Langdales Dictionary of Towns and Hamlets	27
Laurel Road	117
Lawrence Street	87
Lewis, Le Roy, Colonel	15
Library	52, 124, 125

Page

Lifeboats
    The Brothers 80
    Saltburn 84
    Zetland 26, 31
Lilac Grove 103
Lily Park 112
Lime Road 116
Literary Institute 88, 111, 124
Lloyd, Wilson Rev. B.D. 107
Lobster Inn 17, 41
Lobster Terrace 57
Local Health Board, Criticism of 74
Local Health Board, Kirkleatham 63, 64, 79, 105
Local Health Board, Redcar 45, 49, 55, 64, 66, 105
Locke Park 111
Locke, Colonel T. W. S., J.P. 88, 111
Lord Street 19, 25, 40, 44, 55, 86
Low Farm 100
Lumley Road 87
Luna, Wreck of 69
Lynas Place 44, 55

Magistrates' Court 88
Majestic Cinema, "Bug and Flea" 123
Maple Court 115
Maps — see under town name
Marina Avenue 135
Marine Terrace 48, 56
Markets 11, 120
Marsh House Farm 11
Marske
    Old Spelling 9
    Parish 16
    Marske Hall 29
Middlesbrough News & Cleveland Advertiser
    Report of 1861 49
    Report of 1866 51
    Report of 1878 60
Mayors 121, 129, 132, 141
McClean, Robert, Town Clerk 105, 116
McClean Road 118
Memorial Tank 102
Methodist Meeting House 19
Methodist Church, West Dyke 87
Milbank Terrace 56
Military Camp, Green Lane 98
Mineral Railway 110
Morrison Shelters 130

151

	Page
Mowbray, Mrs., Kirkleatham Hall Housekeeper	99
Muriel Street	86
National School	52
National Service Committee	130
National Service Rally	130
National War Savings	103
Nelson Terrace	56
New Pavilion	70, 128
Newcomen Family, Various Members	15, 52, 53, 63, 115
Newcomen Street (Station Road)	41, 57, 119
Newcomen Terrace	52
Newspaper Report of 1861	49
Newsroom, The	48
Night Soil, Removal of	65
Nixon, Councillor, Mayor	129
Non Co-operation Between Redcar and Coatham	
Amalgamation of Towns	81
Boundary Fence	63
Fire Brigade	65
Isolation Hospital	76
Sanitary Authority	63
Normans, The	10
North Riding County Council	130
North Side	40, 44
North Street	73
North Terrace	48
Northern Echo, Report of 1909	91
Old Pott's Cottage	23
"Optimists"	128
Outhwaite, Private	83
Palace Cinema	95, 107, 127
Pankhurst, Miss A.	90
Pansy Road (Conway Road)	119
Parish Hearse	20
Parish Church, Marske	29
Park Avenue	115
Peace Celebrations	101, 134
Pease, Sir Alfred	89
Perci, de	14
Pevsner, Sir Nicholas	52
Phillipson, Councillor T.	101
Picknett Family	84
Piers	
Coatham	69, 81, 95, 96
Redcar	68, 80, 92, 111

Pier Pavilion	95, 96, 98, 128
Pierrots	70, 85, 93, 96
Piersons Buildings	57
Pierson Street	88
Pig & Whistle	120
Pleasure Park, West Dyke Road	117, 127
Plimsoll, Samuel	51
Police Station	89
Poor House	20
Poor Law Unions	42, 105
Population	
Coatham	16, 32, 38, 57, 63, 83
Dormanstown	120
Kirkleatham	16, 32
Redcar	16, 32, 38, 57, 83, 105
Warrenby	120
Port William, Harbour Scheme	30
Portland Place (Coatham Road)	119
Portland Terrace	56, 73, 120
Post Office, Redcar's First	23, 48
Postlethwaite, Rev. J.	53
Pott's Yard	55
Preventive Service, Coatham	33
Prince of Wales Hotel	55
Privvies, Outdoor (Queen Street)	44
Promenade Extension	91
Promenade	91, 121, 126
Public Air Raid Shelters	130
Public Lavatories	91
Punch & Judy	128, 135
Pybus Place	55
Queen Hotel	55, 84
Queen Street	36, 44, 128
Queen Victoria, Death of	83
Racecourse	67, 98, 100, 111, 120, 132
Railway	34, 56
East Halt Station	112
Excursion Trains	135
Extension to Saltburn	36, 58
Footbridges	87
Narrow Gauge	36
Railway Cottages	119
Railway Hotel	40
Railway Terrace, Redcar	73, 119
Railway Terrace, Coatham	41
Ranger Report on Health Standards (1855)	43
Raughton, Wm., His Will	12

	Page
Reading Room	52
Red Barns	57, 99
Red Cross Hospital	99
Red Lion Inn	19
Red Lion Street	73
Redcar	
Coat of Arms	5
Cricket Club	111
Gas Company	104
Iron Works	104
Markets	11, 120
Municipal Borough	105
Old Spellings	9
Parish Church	28, 103
Plan of 1815	19
Plan of 1855	37
Plan of 1861	48
Plan of 1893	71
Population	16, 32, 38, 57, 83, 105
Unemployment (1921)	108
Urban District Council	104
Redcar & Cleveland News, Report of 1902	86
Redcar & Saltburn News	
Report of 1901	86
Report of 1906	87
Report of 1903	91
Report of 1909	95
Redcar as a Resort, Criticism of (1864)	49
Redcar as a Resort, Newspaper Report (1861)	49
Redcar Lane	110, 121
Redcar Parish Church	45, 103
Regent Cinema	70, 127
Regent Place	73
Regent Street	73
Respirators	130
Richmond Road	117
Ridley House (Library)	125
Ridley Street	57
Rivers Estate	116
Robinson, Dr.	132
Robson, Maynard & Co.	61
Rocket Brigade	81, 84
Rocket Terrace	41
Roebuck, Councillor J.	
Rollerdrome	112
Romans, The	9, 36
Roman Catholic Church	62, 87
Roseberry Square	100
Royal Hotel	48

	Page
Royal Munster Fusiliers	98
Royal Naval Air Station	100
Rural District Council, Guisborough	105
Sacred Heart Church, Roman Catholic	62, 87
Sailors & Soldiers Association	101
Salmon Fishing	33
Salt Water Scheme	89
Sam Paul's Pierrots	96
Sandcastles	93
Sandringham Road	117
Sandy Lane (Broadway East)	119
Sanitary Authorities	63
Sanitary Conditions, John Spears 1885 Report	74
Sanitation	44, 108
Saxons, The	9
Seplyns Chapel	12
Sepulchre's Chapel	13
Severn Road	118
Ship Inn, Redcar	19
Sir Wm. Turner's School (Coatham Grammar School)	53
Skinner, Charles	20
Skinner's Baths	20
Skirton, John	24
Small Pox	66, 76
Smith Street (William Street)	44, 114, 119
Smuggling	33
Snow, Captain, Mace-bearer	107
Society of Friends Meeting House	53
Soppett Street	86
South Terrace	43
Spear's Report of 1885	
Spellman, Councillor	102, 122
Spence's Baths	20
Spring Gardens Estate	117
St. Cyprian's Chapel	13
St. Germain's Church, Marske	20, 28
St. Mark's Church, Marske	29
St. Peter's Church, Redcar	19, 28, 45, 103
St. Peter's Grove	113
St. Sulphon's Chantry	13
St. Sulpitius Chapel	11
St. Vincent's Terrace	73
Staithes Road	117
Stamps Baths	20
Stanley Grove	119
Station Road	119
Station Street	40
Stead Memorial Hospital	73, 123

		Page
Stead, F. Arnold	...	123
Steam Boat Trips	...	32
Steam Roundabout, Problems with	...	93
Steel Works, Redcar	...	104
South Staffordshire (4th) Regiment	...	98
Stirling Road	...	117
Stockton Hotel	...	24
Stray	...	110, 126
Street Names, Changes in	...	118
Submarine Patrols	...	101
Suffragettes	...	90
Susannah, Wreck of	...	35
Swan Hotel	...	25
Swin Inn	...	19
Swimming Baths	...	112
Tees Navigation Co.	...	25
Teesside County Borough Council	...	136
Territorial Army	...	130
Theresa Terrace (Coatham Road)	...	119
Thrush Road	...	86
Thweng, Marmaduke de	...	11, 14
Tod Point Road	...	61
Touchwood	...	110
Town Clerk	...	105, 116
Town Clock	...	85, 131
Towns & Hamlets, Langdale's Dictionary of	...	27
Trafalgar Terrace	...	56, 73
Trip to Coatham, Hutton's	...	17
Trunk Road	...	107, 109, 112
Turner Family	...	14, 15, 25
Sir William	...	15, 53
Turner Street	...	41, 73
Tweddel's Visitors Handbook	...	48
Typhus Outbreak	...	43
Unemployment	...	108, 112
Upleatham		
Ironstone Mines	...	36
Parish	...	16, 40
Urban District Councils	...	82, 104, 105
Vansittart Terrace	...	56, 119
Victoria Terrace	...	56, 119
Victory Teas	...	135
Visitors, Number of	...	93, 95
Visitors Handbook, Tweddel's 1863	...	48
Waddler's Concert Co.	...	96
Walbran's Visitors Guide	...	32

		Page
Walker, Maynard & Co.		59, 104
War Memorial		103
Warrenby		61, 118
Boiler Explosion of 1895		79
Fever Hospital		122
Plan of 1893		72
Population		120
Water Supply		77
Works		132
Warrentown		61
Warwick Road		117
Waterloo Tavern		41
Wellington Place		41
Wells Grove		117
Wells, Private		43
Welsh Regiment		98
West Dike Lane		41
West Dyke Road		73, 86, 113, 110, 120
West Dyke School		98
West End (West Dyke Road)		119
West Terrace (West Dyke Road)		19, 110
Westbourne Grove		73
Westfield Terrace		87
Whitby Crescent		135
White's Directory (1840)		32
Wiles, Corporal Wilson		83
William Street		119
Wilkinson, Private		83
Wilton Place (Albert Street)		119
Wilton Street		73
Windmill, Coatham		41
Windsor Road		119
Women's Unionist Association, Redcar		98
Work House, Guisborough		20
World Far, First		97
World War, Second		130
Wrecks, Effect on School Attendance		47
Amarant		80
Birger		70, 80
Caroline		29
S.S. Cochrane		69
Corrymbus		69
Esk		29
Gertrude		84
Griffin		69
Honoraria		84
Luna		69
Susannah		35

	Page
Yeoman's House, Coatham	24
Yorkshire, Baines Directory of	27
Yorkshire Post, Report of 1911	95
Zeppelin Raid	97
Zetland Family	
Dowager Marchioness	123
Earl of	28, 29, 42, 68, 82
Lord	26, 99, 110, 117, 121, 126
Marchioness	127
Marquess	10, 29, 88, 94, 108, 118
Zetland Lifeboat	26, 31
Zetland Homes	118
Zetland Hotel, Redcar	55
Zetland Park	110, 117
Zetland Place (France Street)	86, 119
Zetland Road	117
Zetland Rooms, Library	124
Zetland School	19, 27, 46, 85, 98
Zetland Square	40